BUST!

A Creditor's Guide to dealing
with failing companies

BUST!

A Creditor's Guide to dealing
with failing companies

Vivienne Young

Pitman Publishing

Pitman Publishing
128 Long Acre, London WC2E 9AN

A Division of Longman Group UK Limited

First published in 1993

A CIP catalogue record for this book can be obtained from the
British Library.

ISBN 0 273 60055 9

Typeset, printed and bound in Great Britain.

This book is dedicated to WJO, RJO, WRO and RJHO without whose inspiration and example it would never have been conceived, and to my entire family without whose support and patience it could not have been written.

CONTENTS

Introduction   *ix*

1 Spotting the first signs of danger   1
Giving credit where it's due • First signs of danger
• The gentle touch or the iron glove?

2 Preventing overdue accounts becoming bad debts   8
Collecting overdue accounts — before they become bad
debts

3 Ten ways of trying to recover your money   13
What is insolvency? • A creditor's first steps • Ways
to recover your money • Professional advice to avoid
the 'domino' effect • Stretching your budget •
Directors' legal responsibilities • The importance of
cash-flow forecasts • Pensions at risk?

**4 How the insolvency laws might work for –
or against you**   40
Administration orders • Administrative receivership
• Corporate Voluntary Arrangements • Members
Voluntary Winding-up • Compulsory liquidation
• Creditors Voluntary Liquidation

5 A layman's guide to the insolvency laws   58
Background to the current legislation • CDD Act
• Insolvency Act • Bankruptcy — the facts
• Partnerships

6 Getting the law to work your way   80
Disqualifying a director • Compensation for creditors
under Section 214

7 Predicting companies that might go bust   92
Predicting which business might go bust • Checking
credit worthiness • Insuring against risk

8 Preventing it happening again   101
Money in the bank! • Retention of title • Proficient
paperwork, professional advice • Personal contact

9 Inside the bank manager's head   107
Your bank — friend or foe? • Banking on a winner?
• The hand that pulls the plug

10 Providing a fairer deal for the creditor   116
Strengthening the creditor's hand • Educate and make
the public aware • Making the legislation more
plausible • Freedom of information • Insolvency's
poverty trap • A need for a new type of incorporation?
• Banking on fair play

Glossary   129

Useful addresses and contacts   135

Index   141

INTRODUCTION

In business there is scarcely a more bitter pill to have to try to swallow than a company that owes you money going bust. Unfortunately, a harsh economic climate means that it is more commonplace than any businessman would like to see.

There are various sources of information to assist directors of companies that are facing insolvency, but little help is available to the beleaguered creditor; as I found out the hard way!

This book is written by a creditor for creditors. It is designed to help businessmen and companies of all sizes to minimise the possibility of having to deal with an insolvent debtor, and to understand their situation and their options should the worst happen.

I'm not quite sure where insolvency falls on the psychiatrist's list of emotional disasters, but from personal experience it must be very near the top. I hope that by reading this book you can short-cut my lengthy quest for knowledge and help on the subject and perhaps gain an insight into what is going on around you and how it affects you.

You may not be able to greatly improve or change the situation, but perhaps you will be able to understand what is happening — and why. It was my intention to produce a readable and easily understood 'layman's guide' to coping with being a creditor of an insolvent company — and to show how to avoid becoming one in the first place. I hope you will agree with me once you have read this book and understand a little more about insolvency, that in this case ignorance is most certainly not bliss.

By providing a little more knowledge and exposure of the subject, I hope that this book will go some way towards promoting higher standards for all those involved in commerce and the more effective use of the legislation available.

CHAPTER 1

Spotting the first signs of danger

GIVING CREDIT WHERE IT'S DUE

If an army marches on its stomach, then a business marches on credit! Most businesses make use of credit facilities and extend credit to their customers at some time — usually on a pre-arranged basis, but sometimes unintentionally simply by their late invoicing or their customer's late payment.

Quite simply, if companies did not extend credit facilities, they would not incur bad debts. If you were able to hand over your product with your right hand, whilst collecting the cash with your left, what a perfect world we would have! Obviously, this is a tremendous over-simplification of a complex sphere of business, but it is worth remembering when you are considering offering credit to a customer. In fact, the most effective method of minimising your bad debt risk is to allow credit cautiously and then only after careful consideration and investigation.

Credit should be offered not as a right, but as an inducement to secure higher and more profitable sales figures, providing a lifeline for the growing company. Sadly, too often this lifeline can become a noose and care is needed to ensure that it does not irrevocably tighten and choke the life out of your business.

By necessity businessmen have to be risk-takers to some degree, but they need to carefully balance those risks against the likely returns and ensure that their credit policy accurately reflects the level of risk that they know their company can accept.

Equally, they must closely monitor their credit customers, either personally or through an internal or external credit control department. Monthly, weekly, or even daily assessments of the debtor lists are invaluable in determining not only the size of a valuable company asset, but also the size of the risk. Whether your system is computerised or is a simple manually operated ledger, it should not be too difficult to ensure that your debtors are listed not only by name, but also by the age of the debt.

FIRST SIGNS OF DANGER

But what are the warning signs that the vigilant credit controller should pick up? The first one is obviously non-payment! Without a doubt, a sudden change in the pattern of payments should be one of the first indicators that there is a potential problem arising. It is therefore a priority that your records are suitably organised, monitored and up-dated so that if this occurs it can be spotted immediately. However, there can be a number of reasons why your customer has failed to settle his account other than being strapped for cash.

If you detect a hard-core of debt building up, examine the pattern for any previous payments made by that customer before deciding what action to take. You might be aware now that there is an amount overdue for payment, but perhaps the debtor is simply trading with you in the same way that he has always traded — it is just that you have recently organised your records and highlighted that his payments are habitually late.

If the terms of the credit account are not being met then you will have to decide whether or not to take action to ensure they are met, but it is quite possible that this debtor is not in any immediate danger of financial collapse. Whether or not you are might, of course, dictate your next steps! However, if it appears that a normally prompt payer has deteriorated into late or non-payments then further investigation of the situation is necessary without delay.

The importance of the personal touch

Regular contact between your credit control department and the customer's accounts department is invaluable and one of the surest ways to keep your finger on the customer's pulse. If good contacts are established, not only should you be better placed to ease the account through any sticky problems, but you should also be one of the first creditors capable of detecting any real difficulties. Perhaps you become aware that the person you normally deal with is being evasive with your queries, or is suddenly attending a lot of meetings and unable to take your calls. These are the sort of danger signals that should at the very least prompt you into making further enquiries about the customer's current financial position.

Unfortunately, however, the staff are sometimes the last to find out that their employer is in financial difficulties, so although it is doubtless extremely advantageous to keep in regular contact, this alone is not enough.

Making further checks

Most companies will make credit checks of one sort or another before the commencement of trading with a new customer, but few have these up-dated unless there is a need for a higher credit limit. Many of the firms that specialise in credit checking constantly update their data on the companies they hold files on — sometimes because of newly-filed annual accounts, judgements or even adverse reports from other companies that are dealing with them. If the stakes are high enough, you should consider re-examining the status of customers if there is even a possibility that their financial situation might have changed for the worse.

There are several important warning signs that should be watched for, and these are usually monitored by credit checking agencies. Perhaps the client is increasing or taking new charges in favour of their bankers. Although possibly a sign of planned and healthy expansion, it could be seen in a totally different light if viewed alongside other factors such as increasingly late payments. It is also advantageous to find out whether your late-payers have recently had any County Court Judgements made against them. The Registry Trust Limited will scan the lists for a charge of £4.50 per name and provide you with a postal reply within a couple of days. Alternatively, you may call at their London office to speed up the service. (See useful names and contacts section).

If you are aware of a major collapse within your sphere of business, it is worth scanning the lists of unsecured creditors to see whether any of your customers might have lost large sums of money to the insolvent company. It could prove to be the proverbial straw on the camel's back!

The 'Corporate grapevine' is another priceless source of information when dealing with bad payers. It is quite possible that the company you have identified as a potential problem is conducting business with other firms in your industry. Ensure that your company reps are not only the sales spearhead of your business, but also its eyes and ears in the market place. 'Off the record' chats with other traders can often help to clarify whether your debtor is indulging in serious delays or defaults across the board, or has genuine reasons for your non-payment.

Equally, the responsibilities of your sales-force can be extended to ensure that they not only make a sale, but that the company is paid; close liaison between your credit controllers and salesmen can often result in problems being averted rather than solved.

To summarise then, the important points to remember when watching for distress signals are:

- ensure that your records — particularly your debtor's ledger — are set-up and maintained in a manner that will enable you to identify any potential problem as early as possible;
- maintain regular contact with your debtors on a one-to-one basis wherever possible;
- constantly gather and up-date information from all available sources on your debtors to give as clear a picture as possible of their current financial situation.

THE GENTLE TOUCH OR THE IRON GLOVE?

When you first establish exactly what your credit policy is, your debt collection policy must be considered as an integral and important part of it. It, effectively, is the difference between an overdue debt and a bad debt.

It should be quite clear to your customers just what your terms of trading are and when their payment is due. You might decide to remain flexible as to exactly what course of action you are likely to follow if these terms are not complied with. This leaves your hands free to act with discretion according to each individual situation as and when it arises.

However, when your credit terms are not adhered to, careful consideration is required. For instance, you might feel it correct to withdraw further credit from a customer who has failed to pay his account. If that customer spends only a small monthly amount with you, then this could be all that is needed to lever him back in line; alternatively, should you lose his business by offending him with your choice of action, then you will not have lost a large proportion of your turnover.

But could you afford to lose the business of someone who may spend many thousands of pounds with you? The fact of the matter is that if he isn't paying you, you can well do without his business. If a large customer shows signs of a change in payment pattern, it is prudent to ascertain his current credit status before extending further credit. Throwing good money after bad is one symptom of desperate trading that often proves disastrous. Continually extending further credit to someone who is already paying badly does not add to your turnover or profitability — just to your problems!

As you can see, personal judgement is a prime factor in the way you collect debts, but this should be set against a basic framework to ensure that your 'hunch' does not over-rule the available facts.

Your in-house debt collection policy might sensibly follow a pattern of six steps, then, with a timescale planned to suit your specific needs.

1 Decide how many days 'grace' must pass before you begin to 'chase' the debt. This should be a short enough period to ensure that the delay does not appear to be too serious either to the debtor or to you.

2 As soon as the debt is the magic number of days late, make contact by telephone if possible. If you have no specific contact there — a name provided either through personal contact or perhaps through one of your staff — then establish on this first call who you are dealing with and ensure that they are the correct person to speak to. A friendly call will often nudge them into action, or can often confirm that payment is on its way.

3 Make a follow-up call a week later — or sooner if the previous

conversation merits — to check the position. This will show your debtor that you are aware of the situation and monitoring it regularly.

4 Send the first written reminder. This should be polite, but firm, perhaps implying that the customer must have inadvertently overlooked payment or may have a query, but also perhaps briefly drawing attention to your terms and conditions. If you pull the punches too much at this stage, the letter will inevitably hit the bin without a second reading. A telephone call a few days later might indicate whether or not any action is being taken to settle the account.

5 Normally, a slightly stronger but equally polite letter might follow within a short period of time. If you sense that the customer is being evasive or unhelpful, it could be wise to try and establish just what his financial position currently is if you do not already know. If it seems that there is an imminent danger of collapse, then short-cut these steps and commence legal proceedings.

6 When you decide that enough is enough, act decisively and quickly.

Many companies now engage the services of a debt collection agency of one type or another as a matter of course. If you decide that it is preferable to have an outside collection service, then establish at the outset exactly what you will be getting in terms of service — and what you will be paying for that service.

Never forget, either, that there not only has to be an ability to pay debts, but also a willingness.

CHAPTER 2

Preventing overdue accounts becoming bad debts

COLLECTING OVERDUE ACCOUNTS – BEFORE THEY BECOME BAD DEBTS

When you change from credit monitoring to debt collection, you have a number of choices as to just how the situation can be tackled. If you operate an in-house section, you should monitor on a fairly regular basis exactly how cost effective this is. The work can be very labour intensive if you are not adequately equipped with the relevant soft-ware, and if you are fortunate enough not to have a large number of errant debtors, you may be able to reduce the cost of debt recovery substantially by using an outside agency.

There are any number of specialised debt collection agencies that handle millions of pounds in debt recovery every year. Some firms will specifically only chase nominated debtors, whilst other firms will offer a complete credit control service if required. You will need to decide what your requirements — and budget — are and cut your cloth accordingly.

Most solicitors undertake a certain amount of debt collecting, but there are many firms that now specialise largely or solely in this field. Those that do specialise tend to establish a new set of ground rules as far as their fees are concerned, knowing full well that their normal hourly rates are not viable or cost-effective to most creditors. They rely on handling large numbers of cases rather than on large fees to make a reasonable return.

Whoever you decide to entrust your debt collecting to, ensure that you have a written schedule of the fees that you will be charged. If it looks as though the matter could possibly become a protracted one, then you could ask to be advised when the accumulating fees and charges reach certain pre-ordained limits. For example, if you were chasing a debt of £5,000, you might ask to be told when you have 'spent' £250 trying to get your money, and then told of every subsequent £50 that is spent on your behalf. You are then able to regulate just how practical it is to continue pursuing an action.

Remember, even if you win your case in court, get judgement and are awarded costs, the costs allowed by the court might not necessarily be as high as those being charged by your legal representative. There is also the possibility that you will be unsuccessful in enforcing the judgement, in which case you would get nothing at all. Enforcement can be an extremely difficult process and often a very expensive one.

The usual format once you 'go legal' — whether you choose to use a debt collection agency or a solicitor — is for an initial letter to be sent by them to your debtor informing him that they have been instructed to recover the outstanding sum due and allowing seven days for payment to be made in full before proceedings commence.

The success rate at this stage is generally considered to be quite good, but you will probably have a fairly shrewd idea yourself in advance as to just how far you are going to have to go with any particular debtor before you are paid; as we have said before, the ability to pay is not the only consideration — the spirit must also be willing!

9

Courting problems

Whether your action is taken via the County Court or the High Court depends to a large extent on the amount of money involved. The limit for a County Court action is generally £5,000 as the Bailiffs are unable to enforce on anything higher than this figure. In the High Court, the Sheriffs take enforcement action once you have gained judgement. However, solicitors will often recommend that claims for any amounts over £1,500 will be better going to the High Court as the costs compared to the potential returns enjoy a better ratio.

If the debt is over £750, you can have a Statutory Demand for payment issued, which gives the defendant 21 days to pay in full before you apply for either a winding-up order if the debtor is a limited company or a bankruptcy petition if it is an individual. The demand must be served personally; at the company's registered office if it concerns a company, or on the individual debtor himself. It is often but not necessarily preceded by a Court Action.

This procedure was introduced by the Insolvency Act 1986, when it was considered by many people to be the best news since the abolition of the debtor's prison as far as debt collection was concerned!

When it was introduced, the Lord Chancellor's department made it quite clear that it did not want to see the process of statutory demands being used simply to frighten companies or individuals into payment. Rather it was a procedure that should not be invoked unless the plaintiff was ultimately prepared to apply for a winding-up order or bankruptcy petition.

Of course, there have been numerous examples of these demands being defended and set aside at great expense to both parties. The matter then has to proceed through the courts anyway and so valuable time and money could have been wasted. There have also been examples of solicitors issuing demands on behalf of clients when they should have been aware that they did not conform to the necessary requirements.

If however there appears to be no defence to a debt, the path may be somewhat smoother, but nevertheless the user of this powerful piece of paper must be prepared to put the debtor's back against the wall of insolvency. Again, this can be an expensive exercise and creditors should always try to satisfy themselves that there are assets or funds available to meet the debt and the costs before making any decisions on the viability of instigating a winding up order or a bankruptcy petition.

Imminent insolvency of a debtor?

If you have reason to believe that you have a debtor teetering on the brink of insolvency then without a doubt speed is of the essence and a Statutory Demand could be the swiftest and surest method of securing a judgement in your favour. It is also possible to apply through the courts for an Order 14 Summary Judgement, which is quicker than the normal court proceedings. For this, you must be able to show that your debtor has no defence against the debt.

Your solicitor should be able to provide you with advice as to your best course of action, and will base this partly on his knowledge of the current length of time you can expect to have to wait before a case comes to court.

If you get judgement prior to any insolvency action, then you can immediately apply for one of two things:

1 *A Garnishee Order.* This is applied to the debtor's bank account and effectively satisfies your debt directly from any funds held therein.
2 *A Charging Order.* If you are aware that your debtor has

a significant asset, you can take a charge on it. This has the effect of securing your interest. It is highly likely that the bank will already have a first charge, giving it priority. If it is a fixed and floating charge, you may come away with nothing at all as this allows the bank enormous scope to collect their dues. However, if there is a surplus once the first charge has been satisfied then you are effectively a secured creditor; you have been successful in scrambling a few steps further up the ladder of hierarchy for creditors should insolvency follow.

To summarise, in addition to your normal credit control policy, you should also define your debt collection policy in broad terms:

- ensure that your credit control section is fully conversant with any current proceedings against debtors and is acting in accordance with company policy in respect of any further dealings with that debtor;
- if you opt for an external collection service, establish precisely what each debt is likely to cost you to recover and satisfy yourself that this is a cost effective amount;
- if you become aware that one of your debtors is likely to become insolvent, take the required action swiftly if you consider you may be able to obtain a judgement prior to the commencement of any insolvency action;
- if you obtain judgement and insolvency seems to be looming, take immediate advice on applying for a Charging Order or a Garnishee Order to secure your debt.

CHAPTER 3

Ten ways of trying to recover your money

WHAT IS INSOLVENCY?

In my ageing Universal English Dictionary, the word 'insolvent' is defined as being 'unable to pay debts, to meet liabilities; bankrupt.' By ironic coincidence, the word that follows this entry is 'insomnia'! In order to stand the best chance of avoiding having to endure these two problems simultaneously, it will be necessary for you as a creditor to grasp the rudiments of your debtor's situation, who you will most likely be dealing with — and just what you can and should do.

Once a company believes itself to be insolvent, there are a number of different actions that it can take with a view to either winding-up and liquidating the company, or perhaps trying to re-finance it and keep it trading. Unless the company is being wound-up in the courts — an action that can be taken, usually by an unpaid creditor or sometimes by the directors themselves — then you as a creditor are likely to find yourself dealing with an insolvency practitioner. The courts themselves will actually often appoint an insolvency practitioner to handle certain cases.

What or who is an insolvency practitioner?

Since the 1986 Insolvency Act, an insolvency practitioner must be a 'person who is qualified to act as an insolvency practitioner in relation to a company'. The idea is that a fit and proper person will eliminate the 'cowboy' element that was evident prior to the 1986 legislation.

He will be licensed by one of seven recognised professional bodies — basically, a small congregation of law- and accountancy-based professional societies and associations — which include amongst others the Society for Practitioners in Insolvency, the Law Society and the Institute of Chartered Accountants.

In the UK as a whole, there are some two thousand licensed insolvency practitioners and (according to a spokesman from the Society for Practitioners in Insolvency) 'they are to accountancy what the Bar is to lawyers'.

The law itself is quite specific about the necessary requirements and qualifications of an insolvency practitioner and stipulates that the individual must not be a bankrupt, or a disqualified director, or a patient within the meaning of the Mental Health Act 1983. He must also be authorised by an approved body. Financially, he must have security for the proper performance of his functions. In the draft bill for the 1986 Insolvency Act, there was a provision to eliminate any possibility of a conflict of interest. Although this was not in fact incorporated in the Act itself, ethical guidelines are produced by various professional bodies. The Insolvency Practitioner's expenses 'properly incurred in the winding-up' are payable out of realisations of company assets ahead of all other creditors with the possible exception of cases of administration. The remuneration is either a percentage of company assets to be disposed of or a fee according to the time spent on the case. In large and complex corporate insolvencies these amounts have been known to run well into seven figures!

A CREDITOR'S FIRST STEPS

Once you are aware that you have an insolvent debtor on your hands, you should ask yourself three main questions:

1 What must I do to safeguard my own personal financial situation, or that of my own company — or both?
2 What steps should I take to try and avoid the same thing happening again?

and of course....

3 Is there anything I can do to recover my money?

Normally, the latter consideration is very much at the forefront of the creditor's mind! Although to a great extent the creditor's options for recovering funds are very limited once insolvency proceedings have begun, there are steps in certain circumstances that can be taken that will often produce results. Equally, it is possible to strengthen your control over the ultimate outcome of the proceedings depending on just what form of receivership or liquidation your debtor is involved in. Immediate action is the keyword under these circumstances — and the acceptance that possession is nine tenths of the law!

WAYS TO RECOVER YOUR MONEY

The various options available to creditors to try to recover funds are as follows:

- Creditor powers — particularly in a creditor's voluntary liquidation
- Charging order (must have been in place prior to insolvency)
- Garnishee (must have been in place prior to insolvency)
- Personal guarantee (must have been in place prior to insolvency)
- Retention of title (must have been in place prior to insolvency)
- Lien on goods
- Access to company assets

- Dealing with new proprietors if business to be sold
- Applying pressure to any third party involved
- Action under Section 214 of Insolvency Act − or threat of action

We will take a closer look in turn at each of these options and the climate necessary for its success.

Creditors' powers

Once a company is declared insolvent your position in the hierarchy of creditors is set. However, this does not mean that creditors have no influence and you should certainly not simply throw your hands up in the air and your proxy vote in the bin. Now is the time for determination and a resolve not to write the matter off. You should be ready to monitor the liquidator every step of the way. Ensure that the liquidator checks that no assets were disposed of prior to his appointment at a value substantially less than they were really worth. The Insolvency Act contains a provision within Section 238 whereby a liquidator can, if at the time of the sale the company was effectively insolvent, apply to the court to have the transaction set aside and the goods restored to the company. There is a time limit for examination of six months between unconnected parties and two years between two associates. Similar provisions in bankruptcy proceedings now make it more difficult for a debtor to conveniently 'transfer everything into the wife's name'.

Another area of concern to creditors can be if directors have shown preference to any particular creditor prior to insolvency. Directors who have given personal guarantees to certain creditors (especially banks) may well have paid these debts off prior to the commencement of formal insolvency proceedings. Clearly, if a director acts in this way, he is putting one creditor in a better position than the others and

Section 239 of the Insolvency Act allows the liquidator to set aside such payments and to recover the money.

The process of finalising a failed company's affairs is a lengthy one and those fortunate creditors who eventually do receive some form of settlement may have to wait several years although the more common period of time is from 12 months to 2 years. The early stages of the liquidation are therefore very important. Carefully scrutinise figures and recommendations whatever the form of liquidation, but it is particularly important if you are involved with a Creditor's Voluntary Liquidation (usually referred to as a CVL).

Of all the forms of liquidation — or receivership — this is the one that offers the creditor the greatest opportunity to influence the eventual outcome, largely because their choice of liquidator is given priority over the shareholder's choice. The members may have selected a particular liquidator because they feel he can be more comfortably 'managed' or perhaps even strung along more easily than others. (As mentioned before, the Insolvency Act established firmly the profession of insolvency practitioner as a remedy to rid the system of the 'cowboy' element that was once evident in matters of insolvency. It has been eminently successful and the profession — which numbers only some 2,000 or so spread amongst probably 100 firms — is held in high regard as a whole. However, there will inevitably be the less efficient, less dilligent, less effective and, sadly, the less scrupulous odd rotten apple tucked somewhere in the bottom of the barrel.) As a creditor, you certainly do not want to find yourself at the mercy of such a liquidator.

An insolvency expert with one of the largest credit insurance companies has told me of several instances where creditors have been able to recover many thousands of pounds from insolvent companies involved in a CVL when initially the member's liquidator had indicated there were no uncharged assets and that there would be no dividend at all. He strongly advises creditors to be determined and positive in attitude and not to give up.

You should be sent notification of a creditors' meeting, which will have been preceded by a meeting at which the members will have resolved that the company is insolvent and has appointed a liquidator. It is vital that you make every effort to attend the meeting and if possible try and get an insolvency practitioner to attend with you. It is quite commonplace for practitioners to attend such meetings to advise and assist a creditor and sometimes on a no-fee basis too, the presumption being that it might result in a case for them — presumably only if the case is big enough!

If you cannot attend the meeting in person, don't be tempted to send your proxy in favour of the Chair. The meeting is always chaired by a director of the insolvent company and you are effectively handing over your voting power to one of the people responsible for the bad debts and failure of the company. His choice of liquidator might be very different to yours.

At the creditors' meeting, a statement of affairs will be presented. This will be a very important set of figures and you will not have had an opportunity of examining them prior to this first meeting. An expert eye at this stage can prove vitally helpful, as will any prior investigation of the company you might have made through, for instance, Companies House, where you will find records, returns and accounts required to be filed by law.

As a creditor, you will naturally be particularly interested in the assets figures, which should show not only the book value but also the current realisable value. You must take into consideration, naturally, that the book value of assets is very likely to be very out of date as it will be based on previous accounts and values can change rapidly — take property prices, for instance, in recent years. It never ceases to amaze me, however, that accountants are so ready, willing and able to pronounce values for assets in accounts that can be so wildly different if they ever come to be realised.

Should you be dissatisfied with these figures, question them! If you have done your homework in advance and scrutinised previous years' accounts — and particularly if you have some specialist help with you — there are many areas to be examined carefully. For instance, if a large director's loan account is suddenly apparent, it could have been constructed purely to give the directors greater voting power as unsecured creditors. This in turn could indicate their intention to ensure their own choice of liquidator who they might perhaps feel is likely to act more favourably towards them than the creditor's choice might.

The creditors' meeting also presents you the creditor with an excellent opportunity to question at least one of the directors of the company, as he will be chairing the meeting. You will be able to force issues into the open, in the presence of the liquidator. It has on more than one occasion been used as an opportunity to highlight ways in which the liquidator has been mislead or strung along by the directors.

If you are owed money by an insolvent company which is part of a Creditors Voluntary Liquidation, you should ensure that:

- you receive the necessary paperwork and proxy prior to the creditors' meeting;
- you make every effort to attend that meeting, with an insolvency practitioner if possible, and do your homework on the company beforehand;
- if you are unable to attend the meeting, you do not send your proxy in favour of the Chair;

19

- you act decisively if you do not consider the member's choice of liquidator to be in your best interests;
- you monitor the steps of the liquidation carefully and pay close attention to the assets and their realisable value;
- you think positive and bear in mind that you are in a stronger position to influence the outcome of the liquidation than the unsecured creditors of any other form of liquidation or receivership.

According to the DTI statistics, there are vastly more Creditors Voluntary Liquidations than there are compulsory liquidations. This should raise optimism amongst creditors that they have a good chance of at the very least being able to keep a firm finger on the pulse of the liquidation and hopefully achieving a more satisfactory conclusion.

The down side to this positive thinking is that the creditor holds little sway in any other of the insolvency procedures. It is therefore important to take this into account if you are considering, for example, supporting a Corporate Voluntary Arrangement (CVA). You might decide to resist such a move as you feel that this virtual stay of execution leaves the directors in control of the company (with an insolvency practitioner overseeing) and might perhaps even result in a diminished realisable value of the assets if liquidation does eventually take place. Once the CVA has been accepted it is binding on all creditors and you have no powers to influence the course of events. Equally, if you feel that there is some aspect of the company's trading or the director's behaviour that merits examination, then you should not agree to a CVA, as an examination of the director's conduct is not part and parcel of the arrangement.

Here, once again then, is an opportunity for the creditor to weald a degree of power that might affect the eventual outcome of an insolvent situation.

Having considered the particular circumstances of certain types of receiverships and liquidations, there are additional points that refer to them all.

Charging order/garnishee order

It is only possible to try and recover money from a debtor through court action prior to the commencement of insolvency proceedings. As we have seen in the previous chapter, if you believe a company is about to become insolvent, then obtaining judgement and a subsequent Charging Order or Garnishee Order prior to the actual appointment of a receiver or liquidator can often satisfy a debt, or at least boost your position on the ascending ladder of creditors.

Once the wheels of the insolvency system have begun to move, there is no point in trying to instigate legal action. It may seem frustrating, but consider just how many writs there would be winging their way around the Courts if it were possible to improve the status of a creditor of an insolvent company simply by obtaining a Court Judgement! The theory — and I would emphasise the word theory — of trying to satisfy creditors in a fair and proper manner stems from them all having to play to the same ground rules. In practice, it generally means that the unsecured creditors are all as disadvantaged as each other!

Personal guarantee

It is rarely given, but occasionally if a company requires your services or products badly enough, the directors can be persuaded to provide you with a personal guarantee for payment should the company default. It is not something that they will enter into lightly and you should ensure that the legal documentation is correctly prepared, signed and witnessed.

Obtaining a lien

If you are holding assets of the insolvent company and have been working on those assets — for instance, servicing a company car — you can claim a *lien* over that asset. This gives you a right to hold on to that asset until you are paid or have agreed terms. If this applies to your situation, instruct your legal representative immediately — and hang on to what you've got if you possibly can!

Retention of title

If you have included a 'Retention of Title' in your normal terms and conditions of trading, this effectively enables you to keep title (ownership) to any goods supplied until you are paid in full. Make the insolvency practitioner handling matters aware of this immediately — he is under no obligation to go looking for such things and if he has disposed of any goods before he is aware of the RoT he is not liable. Go to the customer's premises immediately and identify your goods. Insolvency practitioners will advise that you do not remove them, but simply ensure that the insolvency practitioner or his representative agrees and signs a list of the items to which you are claiming the RoT applies. Once you have taken these steps, the insolvency practitioner cannot dispose of these items without your consent. However, the creditor has a substantial task in proving the RoT clause to the insolvency practitioner's satisfaction.

Access to company assets

However, there are also many cases of creditors retrieving goods that have been unpaid for with or without an RoT! Creditors have also been known to 'snatch' debtor's assets in lieu of debts. This is effectively stealing and the insolvency practitioner is empowered to recover such assets. However, there are a lot of creditors out there who have acted in this manner, assuming the right under the reasoning that 'Possession is nine tenths of the law' and have got away with it!

Dealing with new proprietors/owners

Try to establish whether the insolvency practitioner is hopeful of selling the insolvent company as a going concern. On many occasions, the directors themselves have actually purchased the goodwill or contracts attached to the company and begun trading again almost immediately. If there is going to be a continuation of some sort, whether in a new name or in the original format but with a new owner, you could be in a position to negotiate with these directors. If you are able to supply them with a commodity or service that they would have difficulty obtaining elsewhere, you may be in a position to push for 'compensatory' terms to lessen your previous loss and to cover the risk of a similar thing happening again.

If you consider such a course of action, ensure that you take all the available steps to check out their viability just as you would for any new customer, or simply insist on operating the trading account on a pre-paid basis until you are satisfied that they merit a credit account.

Seeking payment from a third party

If there is a third party involved in the business that you have conducted with the insolvent company, take legal advice on the possibility of seeking payment from that third party. This situation sometimes arises when suppliers are dealing with an intermediary who is responsible for a larger contract or project. Much will depend on the contract you have entered into and this course is unlikely to be successful as the insolvency practitioner will be demanding that all debts due to the insolvent company be paid to him. But if there are several creditors in this same situation, the cost of legal representation could be shared and it might be possible to show that as the third party has directly benefited from the efforts of the creditors, there is a responsibility to care for these creditors. It would be a difficult and expensive course to follow, but is nonetheless worthy of consideration.

Action under Section 214 of the 1986 Insolvency Act

Finally, since the 1986 Insolvency Act, there is now legislation that makes it possible — theoretically — for creditors of limited companies to be paid from the personal assets and funds of company directors if certain circumstances prevail. It was always possible for compensatory awards to be made if directors were found to have been acting fraudulently, but this was a very difficult (and expensive) thing to prove, with very high requirements of evidence.

Section 214 of the Insolvency Act introduced the term 'Wrongful Trading', which is examined in greater detail in later chapters. Briefly, it states that if the directors continued to trade after the time that they knew or should have known that the company was insolvent, and that they did not act to minimise the risk to the company's creditors, then they have been wrongfully trading and can be made to contribute personally to the assets of their company, thus theoretically boosting the possibility of a dividend to creditors.

There are inherent problems with this area of the legislation and it has meant that there have been only a handful of cases bearing fruit. (In fact, there have only been a handful of cases brought — although I have been advised by several insolvency practitioners that directors have 'voluntarily' contributed to their company assets when it has been explained to them what could happen if they didn't!)

Not only can it be difficult to define the director's actions as being in direct contravention of this section, but of course it is only worth pursuing them if they have any money! This course of action can only be followed by the liquidator and he will generally seek some form of financial underwriting from the creditors to ensure his costs are met.

This area of the legislation should not only have discouraged directors from putting their creditors at risk if there was a likelihood of insolvency, but it should also have provided some financial compensation to creditors if the worst did happen. It is, unfortunately then, a glimmer of hope in the distance for the frustrated and out of pocket creditor but, until the legislation is tightened up — if ever — it it not something to hold your breath on!

PROFESSIONAL ADVICE TO AVOID THE 'DOMINO' EFFECT

With these immediate priorities taken care of, you must swiftly move on to your own business. Far too often there is a tragic 'domino' effect when a company — particularly a large one — becomes insolvent. Many thousands of good businesses have been ruined, and lives shattered, by the failure of one big company. It is very important that you assess your situation immediately and act accordingly.

In the recession that stalked the early part of the nineties and the tail end of the previous decade, the numbers of business failures increased dramatically with each successive quarter. Figures published by the British Chambers of Commerce on behalf of the Department of Trade and Industry showed that during the first two quarters of 1991 a total of 11,055 companies became insolvent. This represents over 73 per cent of the total number for the whole of 1990 — which in itself was a staggering 43 per cent up on 1989 figures.

Personal bankruptcy statistics are also extraordinarily high for the same periods. I have always been a believer in the old saying that there are 'Lies, damned lies and statistics', but however you look at these figures they are devastating. In the early days of the recession, it was said that tougher times sort out the 'wheat from the chaff' and eventually provide a more streamlined and efficient market-place. Unfortunately, these tough times have been so prolonged that even the largest companies have discovered that there is no-one too big to take a tumble.

Looking at the whole financial situation

As soon as you are aware that you have an insolvent company debtor on your hands, it is essential that you look realistically at your whole financial situation, whether that includes a company, a partnership or simply your own personal bank account.

As we have seen, exactly what steps you should take in relation to your debtor can depend very largely on the type of insolvency they are facing. However, there are steps that you should take immediately concerning your own business and finances, irrespective of the circumstances of the outstanding debt.

The obvious, standard advice meted out is, of course, to contact your accountant and your solicitor. Naturally, it is sensible to discuss such problems with someone from the worlds of accountancy and law, but think carefully whether or not your current professional advisers are really capable of giving you the best and most up-to-the-minute advice on how to manage the problems that you may have to face.

For instance, if you are a very small business or perhaps a sole trader, your accountant might be little more than a glorified book-keeper. He is probably a more than adequate and an economic asset to your business under normal circumstances, but is unlikely to have anything more than a superficial knowledge of the laws and practice of insolvency.

Likewise, your trusted family solicitor probably has proved himself time and time again on everything from conveyancing to making a will; but the new laws that now govern insolvency have only been in force since 1986 — which in legal terms is a relatively short period of time — and precedents are still being established in this complex field of law. Many small firms of solicitors will have had little or no experience with the new law and may struggle to grasp the quite radical new concepts that have been introduced, working with one eye on the problem and one eye on their text book.

Even if your company has an 'in-house' legal department, there may be an outsider far better placed to guide your company through the insolvency maze. I am not advocating that you do not discuss the situation with your normal advisers, merely suggesting that you should be aware that on this particular occasion they may not be the very best placed to guide you through the specific problems that could and do arise when dealing with an insolvent debtor; at the very least their advice might need specialised supplementing from an additional source.

A number of the larger accountancy practices have an insolvency practitioner — or several — on their permanent staff. Quite often, they will form an almost separate though associated 'limb' of the firm. The same is true within a number of law practices, and is in fact a commonly accepted principle with a partner often specialising in a particular field — say, divorce or criminal law — and rarely handling cases other than in that chosen field. The lawyer might be an insolvency practitioner himself, or simply have handled several cases concerning the 1986 legislation. In either case, he is probably extremely well placed to advise and guide you.

Personal recommendation is generally an excellent way of contacting a suitable practitioner. Failing that, there are various professional associations included in the useful contacts listed at the end of this book.

Beware of the insolvency bandwagon!

Do exercise caution if you decide to approach any of the many individuals and firms that have sprung up in the classified 'business to business' columns of the broadsheets during the recession. It seems that many have taken the opportunity of clambering on the insolvency bandwagon and offer what some have described to me as a 'crisis management' service.

I have telephoned quite a selection under the guise of being a potential client and found rather a cross-section of characters: one was a firm of credit brokers, one was a lawyer, and one an accountant. The remainder seemed to be casualties of insolvency itself, keen to provide others with the benefit of their knowledge gained through hindsight. None were licensed insolvency practitioners – although one gentleman informed me that 'effectively, I am'! Another proudly told me that I would be better off not speaking to an insolvency practitioner at all as 'they only, by law, worked for the benefit of the creditors.' Again, here was someone who had either never read the current legislation or simply chose to disregard it.

Perhaps your first decision, even before consulting a professional advisor, should be:

'Should I try to save my business?'

If your answer is in the affirmative, and you succeed in doing so then you should use the experience to learn the answer to:

'Why did it happen?'

Be honest – it could have been poor management in the first place. Whatever the reasons, you can use the knowledge to help your business grow in competence and confidence.

Examine carefully the strengths and the weaknesses of your company. Know where you are making money, and what is costing you profit.

If you are suffering from a liquidity crisis, is it because of unprofitability or cash flow difficulties? If your profitability is in question, then in the short-term you will probably need to inject more capital into the business whilst your long-term problems are sorted out. You could find that you can do this by chasing up your own debtors. A detailed examination of your debtors by age of debt as well as name and amount will soon reveal where the major problems are.

STRETCHING YOUR BUDGET

Many businesses have contingency plans held in abeyance in case the need arises for additional finance. If you have applied it correctly, your overdraft facility should suffice for short-term fluctuations and interruptions to the normal cash-flow process. It should be used for interim support, rather than as a semi-permanent crutch. Beware of relying on its presence as the very fact that it is repayable on demand makes you vulnerable.

Ensure that you always work within the agreed limits and terms of the overdraft − it is extremely unlikely in a harsh economic climate your bank would allow you to do otherwise! If you have operated the overdraft sensibly, then you should find sympathetic handling by the bank should an extra-ordinary need arise.

Factoring or invoice discounting is looked at more closely at a later stage and cannot be discounted as a potential source for finance.

Less orthodox methods

In addition to the traditional sources of finance, there are many less orthodox areas that can be explored in times of need. For example, you may be able to stretch the terms you enjoy from your creditors without jeopardising any future dealings with them. Scrutinise all the statements and invoices you receive and query promptly any that you dispute. This procedure is commonly employed to provide a legitimate reason to delay payment.

Perhaps you could suggest staged payments with specific dates. An early part-payment can often smooth the path for such an action. Post-dated cheques are often another acceptable solution, but you must exercise caution when issuing a cheque if you have any doubt that there will be funds available at the bank to cover the amount. Remember that quite often the clearing banks will not regard any cheques deposited to your own account as usable, cleared funds until several days after you have actually paid them in.

Your creditors may well begin to bring pressure to bear if they learn of a crippling bad debt. Here, careful handling to avoid the domino effect rippling through your industry is paramount. Without panicking your supplier or other creditors, it can be good policy to keep them in the picture and discuss terms of settlement with them before the final red letters become solicitor's writs. You will probably find they are willing to listen to any constructive suggestions that might ease both your situations.

If you are a sole trader or in a partnership, you might find creditors a little more tolerant as they will be aware that you are not protected by a limited liability as is a company director. (This means that when a limited company 'goes bust' the creditors will usually have little or no recourse on the directors of that company, whereas an individual will have to take responsibility for his debts.)

However, if they feel you are about to crumble financially, they may be keen to be the first through the door with a statutory demand for payment. Should this happen to you, take all the documentation to your solicitor without delay as unless the demand is met or is set aside, you could face a petition for personal bankruptcy.

Other unorthodox sources of 'unofficial' credit need to be explored and handled with extreme care. For instance, if you charge VAT on your goods or services and are then holding the taxes you have collected, you could find those funds in your possession for up to four months as the returns are quarterly and then have to be filed within one month. At the very least, if those monies are held on deposit you have the interest that they accrue.

Equally, if it is feasible to do so, try and issue your own invoices at the beginning of the period rather than at the end as it allows you more time to collect the debt – as well as accrue interest! Remember, once you have raised a VAT invoice, that tax is due in the next return whether or not you have received payment.

Likewise, it is plausible and legal to make use of any funds you may have set aside for the payment of Corporation Tax. Normally, there is a lag of up to nine months from the relative year ending before this is demanded.

Tacky, desperate and dangerous
For a labour intensive business, a further source of credit can be found in the deductions made from staff wages. These deductions have to be forwarded monthly to the Collector of Taxes within fourteen days from the end of the tax month. This can give you interest free credit from monies deducted from employees of some three to four weeks.

However, although not illegal, these tactics are tacky, desperate and dangerous both cosmetically and financially. If you mess it up there are severe penalties and the whole concept seems to have Maxwellian connotations! Perhaps a safer use of these monies would be to place them on deposit and off-set the interest raised there against the interest you have to pay on bank borrowing.

DIRECTORS' LEGAL RESPONSIBILITIES

If you are a director of a limited company, then without doubt you and your fellow directors must now look very carefully at your future prospects. If a realistic forecast can be made showing a likely recovery from the present financial crisis by continuing trading, then keep details of this on file for future reference should they ever be needed as proof of the company's aspirations, viability and solvency. This could be necessary for your own protection from liability under the Insolvency Act. Show the basis of your projections and any relevant calculations.

If you are in any doubt as to the continued viability of your business, the advice of an insolvency practitioner could be sought confidentially and without any obligation to act on his advice or recommendations. He will not force you to put your company into receivership or to cease trading; that will be your decision (or possibly a creditor's if things are bad). Either way, his report will be confidential and for your eyes only.

There are avenues now open for companies, in consultation with insolvency practitioners, to pursue that aim to nurture a basically healthy company through a sick period. Hopefully once out of intensive care, it will return to a successful trading pattern without the loss of jobs or creditors' funds so often associated with a failed business. These options are looked at closely in later chapters, as are the implications of 'wrongful trading'.

Wrongful trading

It is perhaps appropriate at this point, however, having just discussed the viability of continuing trading under difficult circumstances, to mention this new term within the field of insolvency and to caution you about its implications.

In 1986, two Acts of Parliament that are very relevant in the context of this book came into force. One concerns the Disqualification of Directors and the other is known as The Insolvency Act. They were effectively the first really big shake-up of the laws relating to this subject for about a hundred years and were formulated after great discussion, debate and detailed reports of, for one, the Cork Committee.

I am not a lawyer and I am not about to report on the legal technicalities as they apply to the Law profession. There are several tomes available through the library service, which provide a very detailed and technical insight into the legislation. (Don't, however, expect one to be readily available on the shelf of your local library. They generally have to be requested — check the library catalogue for what is most current. Failing that the Law Society can usually recommend a suitable title.)

However, these relatively new laws have theoretically made radical changes to the responsibilities of company directors and as such should be studied, digested and never forgotten by anyone who is a company director or could be classed as a shadow director (such as an advisor, or someone who is instrumental in decision-making within the company).

Previously, for a director to be disqualified, it was necessary for a court to prove that he had been guilty of 'fraudulent trading'. In fact, this type of action would often run simultaneously with a criminal prosecution and required similar levels of evidence. Since 1986, there are several other types of unfitting conduct that can result in disqualification proceedings. Directors need only to be found to have been 'wrongfully trading', which is described in Section 214 of the Insolvency Act as meaning:

a) The Company has gone into insolvent liquidation
b) At some time before the commencement of the winding up of the company, that person ought to have concluded that there was no reasonable prospect that the company would avoid going into insolvent liquidation.

The court can make an order for the director to contribute to the company's assets for distribution to creditors in such cases – and it has been done! Following chapters will deal in more detail with this subject and will outline the sort of steps you as a creditor might want to take if you feel that the directors of your debtor company may be guilty of such trading. Meanwhile, consider the implications of this with reference to your own trading position.

If you are seeking guidance from a professional, then it is obviously important that they have as much detail of the overall situation as possible. So much will depend on the type of receivership of the debtor company, and of course on the type of creditor you are.

Again, advice from an insolvency practitioner to help you evaluate your precise position as a creditor can be invaluable. Although they are more usually employed in the business of liquidating a company, most will gladly advise individual creditors on their standing and are engaged in this capacity on occasion.

However, don't necessarily expect any advice from the insolvency practitioners who are handling your debtor. They may be acting primarily to secure the best interests of a debenture holder prior to a liquidation and may not feel any obligation to give you assistance at all.

Help from trade associations
If you belong to a trade association or organisation, then it is certainly worth a phone call to find out if they can help you at all with literature or perhaps counselling. The Institute of Directors, for example, has some six or seven specialist counsellors who are available for consultation by members on a wide range of subjects, including insolvency. However, meetings are by appointment only and you could find yourself waiting a couple of weeks for a timed appointment.

The Federation of Small Businesses is another organisation that is able, amongst many other things, to offer guidance and advice to members facing difficulties in business. They describe themselves as a campaigning pressure group which exists to 'promote and protect the interests of all who are either self-employed or who own or are directors of small businesses'. They have a booklet available for their 50,000 members to provide guidance if they are facing insolvency and although a little out-dated, it provides some practical information.

The chances are that your funds are going to be stretched to the limit because of your debtor, and quite naturally the thought of chucking more hard-earned cash down the same hole grates. Without a doubt, professional fees are not cheap but it is crucial that you are properly advised as to the likely course of events and final outcome at a very early stage.

The Citizens Advice Bureau
The Citizens Advice Bureau is an excellent source of help and have confirmed to me that they generally have an insolvency practitioner 'tucked away somewhere' who can be called upon to provide advice and counselling where necessary. Obviously, each branch will use different personnel, so

do ensure that you are privy to the sort of specialised advice that your situation will merit.

The CAB find that they are dealing with debtors as opposed to creditors more often, and have developed an exhaustive information system that is kicked into gear as soon as a client's problem is identified. If you can see that your own personal finances are going to be badly affected as well as your business, then the help and guidance that the CAB are able to provide can be invaluable. Even just knowing that there are many, many thousands of others going through similar problems can be quite reassuring, particularly to someone who is not used to being in debt.

They have a financial planning fact sheet, *Dealing with Debt*, which is just 25 p — or free if your situation's that bad! I have always found the telephone lines permanently busy, and a vast queue in the waiting room, so it could be a real time-saver if you drop them a note asking for an initial chat on the phone, perhaps to arrange an appointment with their specialist on your particular problem.

If the outstanding debt is substantial enough to throw your business into real jeopardy, then it is important that you take steps straight away to measure the extent of the damage and plan for the immediate future. It is vital that partners — business or marital — co-directors, and accountants, are also aware of the necessity to recognise the best way to tackle the impending problems your business might be faced with. It could mean a minor adjustment to accounting such as restructuring the invoicing system to ensure that all your accounts, or a large proportion of them, are paid within a shorter period of time, thereby speeding up your cash-flow. It might mean a cap-in-hand visit to the bank to apply for extended credit facilities, a larger overdraft facility or a business loan.

Whatever is needed, tackle it head-on; the 'ostrich

syndrome' of simply burying your head in the sand in the hope that things will go away has long been recognised as one of the worst enemies of the troubled businessman!

Once you have taken everything into consideration, if you believe that your business cannot continue having sustained such a blow, then do not be afraid to act on this and take immediate, considered action. To struggle on for a period of time may not only be fruitless and lose you more money, but may also mean that you are risking punitive legislation against you personally if you are a director of a limited company, as we have seen previously.

To summarise, your first steps to protect your own position should be:

- consider whether your company should be saved, if that is possible;
- instigate the necessary action to begin this process if it is considered appropriate;
- take specialist advice from your chosen source – and act on it immediately;
- pay great attention to your own, personal status particularly with regard to the insolvency laws.

THE IMPORTANCE OF CASH-FLOW FORECASTS

Inevitably, one expression that will ring in your ears now if you seek to promote the viability of your business, whether it comes from your accountant, your bank manager or your other advisers, is 'cash-flow forecasts'. Most businesses like to say that they can project fairly accurately on this front and will prepare them on a regular basis as a normal part of their accounting procedure. However, sales and profit forecasts can be dashed with just one bad debtor, so that in a depressed marked the crystal ball is probably only marginally less reliable than cash-flow forecasts. However, they do at the very least provide some outline guide to your corporate expectations, which will be appreciated by your bankers and will help you to plan ahead. As always — but now with an even keener eye — you must examine those figures realistically and with the help of your advisers assess what is your best course of action.

If you are one of the growing band of traders — perhaps within a beleaguered industry such as construction — where you are unsure of your work-load from one week to the next, this is not so simple. Nevertheless, there are certain groundrules that can be used to form your forecast.

You may be advised by the insolvency practitioners handling the insolvent company that owes you money, that there will be a dividend (percentage payment) paid to all unsecured creditors. They will probably initially be able to suggest only an approximate figure and indeed will have some difficulty in predicting any timescale this might fall within, as much will depend on the speed at which any assets are disposed of and obviously for how much. In any event, try to ascertain even an approximate amount and a date, so that this can be incorporated into your cash-flow forecast.

If you have a hard-core of existing orders or contracts, no matter how apparently small or insignificant, then don't just include this in your current turnover, but also build your projections around this. If possible, show the sort of average turnover enjoyed for the past six, twelve or twenty-four months and indicate how closely you expect the future trading pattern to adhere to these levels. Try to allow for seasonal changes and anticipated price increases, and be as realistic as possible.

A careful analysis of your expenditure should show clearly your necessary overheads and the levels they are expected to reach (for example, your rent or mortgage, rates, hire purchase, power etc). There will be many variables over the next few months; for instance, will you be able to forecast accurately what your wages bill will be when you know that you may find yourself forced to lay staff off? The number of vehicles you will be operating might vary dramatically. Again, with the help of your accountant if necessary, draw up a plan that will show these as realistically and honestly as possible. Bank managers hate to be treated as mushrooms — kept in the dark and fed something the cattle left behind!

PENSIONS AT RISK?

Finally — although I suppose technically not construed as such — you could consider yourself to be a creditor of an insolvent company if you were one of its employees and were in an occupational pension scheme.

If your employer goes into insolvent liquidation it is extremely unlikely that your pension will have been affected adversely. Despite the headliners such as the Mirror Group, most pension funds are left intact and unplundered by company directors and pensioners receive exactly what is due to them.

If you are confused or need reassurance concerning your pension, you should first approach the Trustee who will have been responsible for the pension fund. Since the 1990 Social Security Act, the liquidator of an insolvent company must appoint an independent trustee, who then works to administer that fund to the best of his ability.

If you are still concerned, then Occupational Pensions Advisory Service (OPAS) (see 'Sources of Information') are a font of information and are quite used to weaving their way around the maze of pension and trust law.

CHAPTER 4

How the insolvency laws might work for – or against you

In this chapter, we will take a slightly more detailed look at the various procedures that companies can use to cope with their insolvency. My main purpose here is not to go into lengthy legal rhetoric about the infinite details and differences of these procedures; it is simply to try to clarify any significant points that might affect the creditor and the actions he should take to best safeguard his own interests and those of his business.

ADMINISTRATION ORDERS

This is a new procedure introduced by the 1986 legislation, whereby a court can make an 'Administration Order' with regard to a company in financial difficulties. The company is placed in the hands of an administrator – an insolvency practitioner – and while the Administration Order is in force, that company cannot be wound-up or proceedings be enforced against the company without the leave of the court.

For the court to make such an order, it must be satisfied that the company is unable to or likely to become unable to pay its debts and that such an order would be likely to achieve one or more of the following:

● the survival of the company in whole or part;

- approval at a meeting of the company and its creditors of the composition of a scheme or arrangement concerning the company's affairs and debts;
- the sanctioning under the Company's Act of a specific compromise or arrangement;
- a more advantageous realisation of the company's assets than if the company were just wound-up.

Clearly, the prime purpose of an Administration Order is to try and hold a business together so that it can either be rescued or the best return on its assets gained.

As the creditor of a company that is hoping to have an Administration Order placed on it, you must consider straight away whether you consider it viable for the company to be handled in such a way.

Do you feel that the main reason for applying for such a process, which can mean a longer more protracted battle to realise your monies, will benefit you? Or do you feel that a more advantageous figure can be achieved for the assets if an Administration Order is made, therefore giving you a better chance of getting more of your money? Then again, do you feel that the main reason is for the long-term survival of the company, which might or might not benefit you directly?

You have only a limited amount of time to decide whether you wish to reject the entire principle and apply immediately for a winding up order against the debtor in the court, or wait to attend the various meetings that will ensue once an order is granted, if that is the case.

A petition is lodged with the court that will include various affidavits, statements and other relevant details. A statement of the company's financial position, listing its assets and liabilities and detailing security held by creditors is provided, which may make interesting reading — and at least saves you the time, expense and bother of investigating this aspect of the company via Companies House. A report may also be lodged in support of the petition, usually by an independent person who has adequate knowledge of the company's affairs or perhaps the proposed administrator. This report should point out that the appointment is expedient and specify which of the purposes (as noted above) an Order is likely to satisfy.

At the hearing, there are any number of people entitled to be present or represented, and although unsecured creditors are not specifically mentioned, allowance is made for the court to give leave for 'any other person who appears to have an interest'.

The court can dismiss the petition, adjourn the petition or make the Order. If the Order is granted, the administrator advertises the notice in the *Gazette* and such other press as he considers to be appropriate to catch the eye of the company's creditors. He must also send written notice within 28 days of the Order to all the creditors of the company that he is aware of.

Once this happens, then the company is effectively under the wing of the administrator and matters follow a pre-ordained course of action.

The Administration Order in practice

The administrator now has three months to prepare and propose a plan to try and achieve the desirable ends specified in the Order, whether this is for the rehabilitation of the firm or the most profitable realisation of the company's assets. Often he will try to keep the company's business turning over to enable him to sell the business as a going concern. During this time, the administrator will manage all the affairs of the company in accordance with any directions given by the court; if and when the proposals are approved, he then manages the company in accordance with those proposals.

The court can allow for a longer period, but generally speaking after three months a statement showing the administrator's proposals to achieve what he was appointed to achieve will be ready, together with:

- details of his appointment;
- its purpose and any subsequent variations;
- names of the directors and secretary of the company concerned;
- account of the circumstances which gave rise to the application for an Administration Order;
- copy of statement of affairs and administrator's comments if any or if no statement submitted, then details of the financial position of the company at the last practicable date (usually not earlier than the date of the Administration Order);
- any other information concerning the running of the company's affairs should the proposals be approved and which may help creditors to decide whether or not to vote to adopt the proposals, should also be included.

The creditors' meeting

To vote at a creditors' meeting, you must have provided the administrator by noon the preceding business day with written details of the debt you are claiming. Obviously, the more proof you can show here – within reason – the better. The creditors' 'clout' as to their voting ability is calculated on the balance of debt due.

The meeting can vote to accept the proposals in all or part, suggest revisions or refuse to approve proposals at all. If the meeting does reject the proposals, the court can do one of many things, including discharging the order, adjourning the hearing conditionally or unconditionally or making an interim order as it sees fit.

If the meeting approves the proposals, it may wish to establish a creditors' committee whose function is to assist the administrator — but of course, can also be of great help and reassurance to the creditors.

During the Administration period, the administrator must provide a progress report every six months along with various other data including details of all receipts and payments. There is no specific criteria as to a timescale for this overall procedure but the administrator by virtue of his appointment will take every step to ensure a satisfactory conclusion is reached as swiftly as possible.

The administrator's powers

His powers enable him effectively to do all things necessary 'for the management of the affairs, business and property of the company' and more specifically he can raise or borrow money, appoint solicitors or other professionals to assist him, transfer business of the company to subsidiaries and even employ or dismiss employees.

If you are dissatisfied with the way the administrator is handling the affairs of the company and believe that this is unfairly prejudicial to the interests of its creditors or some of the creditors, then you can petition the Court accordingly. As in all matters of business, it is vital that you and your own selected 'experts' — be they accountants, solicitors or perhaps insolvency practitioners themselves — study carefully each stage of the proceedings and monitor the success or likely success of the administrator very closely.

There is a significant drawback to this apparently admirable attempt to see fair play for creditors whilst helping with the survival of a business wherever plausible: the cost. Generally, only the larger companies are suited to this arrangement as large, five figure sums are inevitably involved — and have to be paid by a company that is theoretically insolvent!

I have heard figures of £50,000 minimum costs mentioned in respect of Administration Orders; no doubt, there are many instances to disprove this, although I suspect that there are many more that will back it up.

One of those amusing footnotes to the British system of law and order is contained within these sections of the Insolvency Act, which states that should the administrator die, he will only be released from his position from the time at which notice of death was given to the court; you could then, in effect, have a dead administrator in total control of a company and all its assets for a short period of time!

ADMINISTRATIVE RECEIVERSHIP

The 1986 legislation introduced this as a new term for what had previously been called a 'receiver and manager'. An administrative receiver is appointed by or on behalf of 'the holders of any debentures of the company secured by a charge which, as created, was a floating charge or by such a charge on one or more other securities'.

Basically, it means that someone with a charge – mortgage – over company assets and/or property (generally speaking the company's bankers) has decided the time is right to realise its security. If it believes that its security is being eroded or perhaps that the company has insolvency problems, then it can appoint an administrative receiver. There is no specific criteria as to why, how or when this can or must be done other than the presence of insolvency, and it is an action taken purely at the discretion of the debenture holder. However, often a report or a detailed examination of the company's situation has led someone to press the 'panic button'.

The duties of an administrative receiver are quite clearly set out; they are primarily concerned with ensuring the realisation of sufficient funds to discharge the company's indebtedness to the person or organisation that appointed the administrative receiver. He will manage the company's affairs and safeguard the assets under his control. He may also be required to account to other secured creditors. He will deal with the company's preferential creditors, but when his task has been completed he will return control of the company's business and assets (if there are any remaining) on to a liquidator, if one has been appointed.

Naturally, everything should be handled in a most ethical and circumspect manner, and if and when a liquidator is appointed then the actions of the administrative receiver will be closely scrutinised to ensure that this has been the case. But do remember that if you are an unsecured creditor, the administrative receiver is not your friend and ally; he may well not be an enemy, but you are of very little consequence to him and he will not be looking to do you any favours.

Depending on the individual's frame of mind and time availability, you may find him helpful. However my own personal experience was of a young gentleman (and I use the word 'gentleman' very loosely) who told me our company was unlikely to see a penny of the six figure sum owing to us, and couldn't even be bothered not to talk with his mouth full as he snatched a quick mid-morning sandwich!

Fixed charges

There is an important difference in the appointing of an administrative receiver according to whether the debt is a floating charge or a fixed charge. In the first case, his duties are discussed later on. If he is appointed because of a fixed charge, he becomes the receiver or manager only of that property so charged. His powers are governed by a separate act – the Law of Property Act 1925 – and he is not required to be a licensed insolvency practitioner. The latter is certainly the rarer occurrence but it is worth noting its existence.

Within 28 days of an administrative receiver's appointment, he must send a notice to all creditors he is aware of. The directors of the company lose their executive powers at the time of the receiver's appointment although they remain responsible for their statutory duties 'in so far as they are able'.

The administrative receiver's powers

The administrative receiver's powers are conferred on him by the debenture under which he is appointed. They include powers specified within the Act and enable him to do a myriad of things, including carrying on the business of the company, taking possession of the company's property, raising or borrowing money, calling up any of the company's uncalled capital, employing or dismissing employees, claiming against a debtor of the company, and also establishing a subsidiary of the company and transferring the whole or any part of the company's business to that subsidiary.

Within three months of appointment – or longer if the court sees fit – the administrative receiver must send a report to a number of people including the registrar of companies, and to all secured creditors, and 'in so far as he is aware of their addresses to all such creditors'. Alternatively, he can publish a notice where he believes the unsecured creditors will see it, stating that they may write to him for free copies of the report.

The report must show the events leading up to his appointment, proposals or details of disposal of property, the amount due to the debenture holder, any amount expected to be available to other creditors, a summary of the statement of affairs that was submitted to him and his comments, if any.

The report does not have to disclose any information that would 'seriously prejudice the receivership'. As the receivership is obviously by the nature of its origins loaded greatly in favour of perhaps just one bank, it is arguable as to the wisdom of such an inclusion. Does it mean that the bank must be allowed an unencumbered 'first bite' regardless, whilst the other creditors, who can only pick at the bones, have no right to full and frank disclosures concerning the overall picture of the company's situation?

The creditors' meeting

A creditors' meeting will be called and the administrative receiver or his nominee will chair this meeting. At this meeting, the administrative receiver sets out a number of facts, including events leading up to his appointment. To vote at the meeting, you must have provided the administrative receiver with written details of the debt and of course any relevant proof of debt to substantiate your claim. This must be in his hands by noon of the preceding business day. Creditors whose claims are wholly secured are not entitled to attend the meeting and therefore certainly not entitled to vote. The voting entitlement of a creditor is calculated according to the debt. A secured creditor may attend and vote if there is an element of the debt that is unsecured. A simple majority voting system is used to pass resolutions. The directors do not have to attend and the meeting is not designed to look into their actions.

The creditors' committee

A creditors' committee can be formed if it is so resolved, and three to five creditors whose claims have been accepted can be elected. The function of the committee is set down as being to 'assist the administrative receiver in carrying out his functions and to act in such a manner as may be agreed from time to time'. It has no power to supervise or direct the administrative receiver and is effectively a toothless lion. I suppose it may give the comfort of believing that you are aware of what is really happening at the sharp end, but I am rather sceptical of the merits of theoretically assisting a man whose prime and often only concern is to discharge the debenture holder. It seems just a little bit like the Christians sharpening up the lion's teeth!

The dealings conducted under the banner of administrative receivership can be very protracted and a requirement is contained within the Act for an abstract of receipts and payments to be made for each 12 month period that the administrative receiver is 'on duty'. Copies are sent to Companies House and amongst others, the members of the creditors' committee.

The question of whether or not it is serving your own best interests to go along with an administrative receivership is impossible to generalise about. Theoretically, the insolvency practitioner concerned must surely obtain the best figures possible when realising the company's assets and although he is doing that to ensure that whoever appointed him receives the amounts due under the charge they have, the end result should still be the same: a realistic price for assets and hopefully a residue to go towards satisfying the other creditors.

The problem can often be that banks tend not to panic until they can see their security is actually diminishing — for example, a massive slump in property prices such as often experienced in a recession. Unfortunately therefore, it is quite common to find that when a sale is forced, the security will only just cover the amount due to the debenture holder.

Take careful, considered advice, preferably from an insolvency practitioner, as to your best course of action. It is of course possible for you to instigate a winding-up order against the company, but apart from the cost involved in doing so, it does not give you any actual preference when the cake is eventually shared out. However, as a petitioning creditor you would perhaps hold a little more sway when it comes to making yourself heard.

Importance of the Report to Creditors

I think it is also very important that you study carefully the Report to Creditors you will be provided with. Certain facts and figures are generally included in this report, but if you want to get a full financial picture, you can apply for copies of recent details filed at Companies House.

It is very tempting to push the report to one side if you already know it is unlikely that unsecured creditors will be paid, but persevere. The more knowledge you have of your debtor and the circumstances that gave rise to the receivership, the better able you will be to tell if you have any real prospect of legal retribution. Also, you will have more chance of identifying another potential bad payer in the future.

Chapter six deals in far more detail with the 1986 Directors Disqualification Act and Section 214 of the 1986 Insolvency Act and it can be useful if you begin to develop your 'nose' for smelling – and pursuing – a rat.

Finally, remember that there is the possibility that once the administrative receiver has fulfilled his obligations and discharged the debt due to the debenture holder, there will still be sufficient assets, goodwill and business remaining to satisfy other creditors. Administrative receiverships do not always precede a liquidation although this is usually the case. Unfortunately, liquidation figures in a recession tend to be heightened by the banks, who not only send in the receivers, but are also reluctant to lend money – even to someone hoping to purchase the remains of an insolvent business from the receiver. A business that still has potential might often be liquidated because would-be buyers are unable to raise the cash. It's the banks' equivalent, perhaps, of the 'Double Whammy' – send in the receivers for their pound of flesh, but don't lend any money to a potential purchaser that might have ensured fewer job losses and a payment for creditors.

CORPORATE VOLUNTARY ARRANGEMENTS

Corporate Voluntary Arrangements (CVAs) are becoming more and more common and can often mean a far better return for the creditor than if the company is simply wound-up. It also means that the company may well continue to trade, which of course implies further business for the creditors and the saving of jobs.

It is basically a legal scheme of arrangement whereby the company proposes to discharge its creditors in part or full over a specific period of time, designed to provide a cheaper and less formal method of restructuring, or possibly winding-up, a company that may be suffering short- or medium-term financial difficulties.

For the insolvency practitioner, the critical hinge of the operation is to be certain he is aware of all the creditors and that they are all made aware of the creditors' meeting. This ensures that if the majority vote to accept the proposals, then no creditor can apply to wind the company up. Whether they chose to attend the meeting or not is irrelevant, it is sufficient that they were informed and had the opportunity to attend.

Obviously if you feel strongly that a CVA is not desirable or in your best interests, then it is important that you make this known by voting at the creditors' meeting.

The successful arrangement

The success of such arrangements can largely depend on the type of relationship the debtor has had with his creditors in the past. If he has had a good, long-standing business relationship with a creditor and it looks likely that the whole situation can be salvaged, then the chances are the proposals

51

will be accepted and perhaps a liquidation is not inevitable. However, a 'dodging' debtor, who has constantly maintained that the 'cheque is in the post', is unlikely to hold much credibility with his creditors now.

It is sometimes impossible to save a business, although a quick disposal of assets might help the creditors. This often happens where the debtor is concerned with some form of contracting as the contracts will generally be determined – cancelled – if the company is deemed insolvent. Many successful and profitable businesses can class contracts and good-will as their most valuable if least tangible assets. Often, once these have disappeared, so has the business itself.

At the creditors' meeting, a resolution to approve the proposal must be passed by a majority of 75 per cent in value of the creditors present, in person or by proxy, and voting. Within four days of the meeting, the Chairman must prepare a report and file a copy with the court. He must also give the results to all those who were sent notice of the meeting – i.e. not just those present – and if the meeting had approved the proposal, a copy of this must also be attached.

During the course of the arrangement, the supervisor is bound to keep records of his transactions and all receipts and payments of money, and he must submit an abstract of the same at no greater than 12-monthly intervals.

Finally, when the arrangement is completed, notice must be sent with full details to all those bound by it. Any differences between the actual implementation and the proposals must be explained in detail.

At the time of writing, suggestions by the insolvency profession are being considered concerning possible improvements to this procedure. They have mooted the point that the ability for them to implement a 'stay' of creditors' actions whilst a voluntary arrangement is being prepared for consideration would enhance the current format.

These three preceding procedures do not necessarily mean the company concerned will inevitably go into liquidation, although, obviously, they often do:

- Administration Orders;
- Administrative receiverships;
- Corporate Voluntary Arrangements (CVAs).

The following procedures mean liquidation is an inevitability.

MEMBERS VOLUNTARY WINDING-UP

If the company you are concerned with is going ahead with a Members Voluntary Winding-up, then you should have little or no cause for concern because to take these steps, the company must be solvent. This means all creditors will be paid in full. It is generally more of a formality rather than a procedure that will leave unpaid creditors in its wake. Relax and just monitor the situation as it evolves, ensuring that your claim − if you have one − has been accepted. The debts, including interest, should be paid in twelve months although any difficulties, such as tax position, can drag matters out for a much longer period.

COMPULSORY LIQUIDATION

A compulsory liquidation or winding-up is a procedure that goes through the courts rather than through an insolvency practitioner. It is generally considered to be a last recourse against an insolvent company that continues to trade despite its lack of funds, when it is considered detrimental to the creditors. It is brought about by petition, usually by a creditor but sometimes by the directors themselves.

There are various grounds for petitioning for the winding-up of a company but the most common is for the non-payment of debts.

Non-payment of debts

The procedure itself begins when a creditor whose debt is £750 or more has served a written demand at the company's registered office and still the company has not paid or secured the debt. The local County Court, or perhaps your Citizens Advice Bureau, will be able to advise you on the precise format that such an action will take and the costs involved. It is worth noting at this stage that the order of priority for creditors of an insolvent company is not changed by or any priority given to the petitioner. It is also worthy of note that if the company has no assets as such, a lot of additional expense could be incurred by the creditor to no avail.

CREDITORS VOLUNTARY LIQUIDATION

A Creditors Voluntary Liquidation is brought about after the directors of the company have considered its financial situation at a board meeting. They resolve that the company is insolvent and should therefore be wound-up and an insolvency practitioner is instructed who arranges for a creditors' meeting to be called. Prior to this he advertises in the *Gazette* and two local newspapers, stating either the name and address of the insolvency practitioner who can supply, free of charge, information about the company's affairs as the creditor might reasonably require, or a place in the locality where during the two business days before the meeting a list of creditors' names and addresses may be inspected.

The directors make out a statement of affairs, verified by affidavit, and this is submitted to the creditors' meeting and to the liquidator when appointed. The shareholders can appoint a liquidator up to fourteen days prior to the creditors' meeting, but he cannot dispose of any assets other than perishables or things likely to diminish in value unless they are disposed of immediately.

A CVL probably gives the creditor more scope to influence the final outcome of the liquidation than any other type of procedure. Once the members have made the resolution that the company is insolvent and an insolvency practitioner has been appointed, the necessary paperwork will be prepared and sent out to creditors as required by law, together with a proxy.

Appointing a liquidator

The members meet and appoint a liquidator, having made their formal resolution. Often they then come straight out into the meeting of creditors. During this meeting a statement of affairs will be presented. The statement will probably contain some fairly depressing reading as far as the company's latest figures are concerned, but if studied carefully can be very revealing.

The important area to watch is the assets figure; there should be a 'book value' as shown in the last accounts and a realisable value. The creditor now has the opportunity of questioning these figures and seeking out just how accurately they reflect the present market. This is generally possible in all liquidations or receiverships. However, the unique aspect of CVLs is that the creditors can vote in their own choice of liquidator if they are dissatisfied with the members' choice.

The following procedures are very similar to those of a compulsory liquidation, with resolutions passed by a majority. Within 28 days of the creditors' meeting, the liquidator must send a summary of the statement of affairs and a report of the meeting to the company's creditors. The power of the company directors ceases with the appointment of the liquidator.

When the affairs of the company are fully wound-up, the liquidator calls a meeting and lays before it the full detailed account of the disposal of assets and the conduct of the liquidation. The creditors may question him on any matter at this meeting. The liquidator has to convene a meeting of the creditors every twelve months to provide a report on the progress of the liquidation.

The plight of the small business

These, then, are the basic outlines of the methods available to companies facing financial problems. I cannot help but feel that there is one very neglected area and one that has increased rapidly in the past decade – that of the small business that is unfortunate enough to find itself insolvent and with virtually no tangible assets.

Because of the expense involved when using an insolvency practitioner, they have very little choice but to apply to the court for a winding-up order. The stigma that has always been attached to this procedure varies little whether it is a petition from a creditor or a responsible director trying to liquidate his business as best he can. The procedure is basically the same and will be scrutinised at every stage by the Official Receiver's office.

Surely, with the number of small businesses failing, often through the 'knock-on' effect of a loss from a larger company going under, it is time for some sort of contingency fund to be established, perhaps through the official institutes and organisations of the professions most concerned in this field, including insolvency practitioners, accountants and lawyers. Administered in a similar fashion perhaps to legal aid, a company's eligibility for financial help to appoint an insolvency practitioner could be established by various criteria including the company's assets. The need for a winding-up through the courts could then be substituted by a less daunting liquidation in the hands of an insolvency practitioner.

In what has become a flourishing industry in recent years, isn't it time that the professionals injected a little compassion back into the non-profitable end of the insolvency spectrum?

Problems and difficulties

Whichever of these arrangements you may find yourself involved with, there are inevitably problems or difficulties one way or another. Creditors often feel short-changed and in practice, they frequently are. It is worth remembering, though, that in the majority of cases the company directors concerned are losing their own livelihoods, and quite often everything else. There will always be the rogues who try to manipulate the laws and the privileges of limited liability to further their own ends, but thankfully they are relatively few in number. The new legislation goes a long way towards minimising, though not eliminating, these types and also encourages directors as a whole to take a more responsible and proper attitude with all the affairs of their company. The next section takes a closer look at this legislation, its interpretation, its application and of course its overall effectiveness.

CHAPTER 5

A layman's guide to the insolvency laws

BACKGROUND TO THE CURRENT LEGISLATION

The legislation that was introduced in 1986 was something of a watershed in matters of insolvency — particularly corporate insolvency — because it introduced the first substantial changes in this field of law for more than a century. As we have already seen, one of the things that it did was to introduce new ways for the handling of corporate insolvency to both simplify and improve the existing methods.

Back in 1962, the Jenkins Committee, who were reporting on Company Law, came to the conclusion that the Companies Act did not 'deal adequately with the situation arising from fraud and incompetence on the part of directors — particularly directors of insolvent companies'. They went on to recommend measures that were apparently seen as far too radical or wide-sweeping, because they were not enacted. They suggested that 'directors and others who have carried on the business of the company in a reckless manner (should be) personally responsible without limitation of liability, for all or any of the debts or liabilities of the company if the court so declares on the application of the Official Receiver or the liquidator or any creditor or contributory of the company'.

At this time, only fraudulent acts were able to be dealt with in this manner and the idea of directors possibly having to dig deep into their personal pockets must have sent shock waves through the more murky lower echelons of trade and commerce. Some major corporate collapses over the next decade or two heightened the public's general dissatisfaction, frustration and even distrust in company law. On the other side of the coin, it also gave grand ideas to those who found it tempting to exploit the gaping loopholes. Many times, directors of failed companies would spring up afresh — within days sometimes — like a new crop of toadstools. Having purchased from the liquidator stock or some other assets of the failed company at a bargain price, they would often have done very well out of their failed business, leaving only the unpaid creditors moaning in their wake.

The only course of action for creditors seeking compensation from the directors personally was to try and prove that they had carried on their business with the intent to defraud creditors. Few creditors found this a plausible course of action however, as the courts tended to look upon fraud as a criminal matter, rather than a civil one.

The Cork Committee recognised these failings, and recommendations that encompassed both an element of the deterrent and an element of punishment were incorporated in the two instruments of legislation we have referred to. Of course, there are many other aspects of these laws and they are far-reaching. There are also certain other relevant sections of law included within the statutes, but for the purpose of this book, we are going to examine specific aspects of the Company Directors Disqualification Act 1986 (for simplicity, I shall refer to this as the CDD Act in the following text) and the Insolvency Act 1986, as these are the most recent and the most likely to be implemented.

THE COMPANY DIRECTORS DISQUALIFICATION ACT

The CDD Act is a compact and fundamentally well-structured piece of work, which theoretically waves the

Sword of Damacles above the heads of errant company directors. It is vastly shorter than the Insolvency Act of the same year and seems to be demanding higher standards from directors as a whole, and a more responsible attitude from those who are directors of insolvent companies.

It makes provisions for directors to be disqualified for a number of reasons, including: conviction of an indictable offence (generally in connection with management or liquidation of a company); being persistently in default of providing returns and the like to comply with current company law; and fraudulent trading (and we've already seen that is a difficult one to enforce). These are largely contained within the first five sections of the Act.

In addition to these and shining through the bog of legal terminology like a beam of winter sunshine on a foggy November morning, comes Section 6. This states that the court shall make a Disqualification Order against a person where it is satisfied that 'he is or has been a director of a company which has at any time become insolvent (whether while he was a director or subsequently) and that his conduct as a director of that company ... makes him unfit to be concerned in the management of a company'.

Section 6 provides for a subjective, considered assessment of an individual's behaviour and as such offers a great opportunity for the courts to regulate far more closely the conduct of company directors. The minimum period of disqualification is two years, the maximum 15 years.

Later in the Act, we also find Section 10. It uses similar terminology to Section 214 of the Insolvency Act and provides for directors who have participated in 'wrongful trading' and have had a declaration made against them under Section 214, to be disqualified for a maximum period of 15 years.

Wrongful trading is a new term introduced by the 1986 Insolvency Act legislation and is examined in more detail later. It seems to have been introduced to allow the courts greater flexibility in judging whether a director's conduct towards his creditors has been fair and responsible.

The statistics provided by the Department of Trade and Industry and published on their behalf by the Association of British Chambers of Commerce, show a sudden leap in disqualifications soon after the legislation, as would be expected. However, it does not appear that the rate of disqualifications is matching the rate of adverse reports on directors submitted by investigating insolvency practitioners. What appears to have happened, perhaps inevitably in a recession, is that a back-log of investigations is accumulating at a rate far greater than the staff within the Insolvency Service at the DTI are able comfortably to cope with.

It is obviously still early days to analyse any pattern and difficult to assess these figures in relation to the number of company insolvencies. However, it is worth noting that at a meeting in mid–1991 between representatives of the Technical Committee of the Society for Practitioners in Insolvency (SPI) and John Redwood, MP then Minister for Corporate Affairs, the Minister reported that some 1,000 Disqualification Orders had been made and another 600 applications were waiting to be heard. It is, perhaps, the numbers 'waiting in the wings' that will determine the overall trend. Inevitably, these cases take some considerable time to be compiled and decisions are not made lightly. The toll of the current recession is likely to roll on for some time yet and the statistics will not be able to be successfully analysed for perhaps five years if a realistic pattern is to be identified.

The SPI made the valid point that although these figures appear to represent a large number of cases, when considered in conjunction with the number of adverse reports submitted, it was low. According to the Insolvency Service, during the period April 1986 to November 1991 some 20,000 reports were received from insolvency practitioners and official receivers citing unfitted conduct by directors of failed companies. In the same period 2,159 applications for disqualifications were made. Without a more detailed breakdown of the period in question and a longer period to sample it is impossible to make sweeping assumptions, but set against any criteria the actions will be likely to appear on the low side. Apparently, the Minister agreed to review the level of applications to see if any improvements should be made.

Disqualification periods

The length of periods of disqualification are categorised in varying bands of time, from under one year to between ten and 15 years. (See table 5.1). Each year to date, more disqualifications seem to have fallen in the period of over four but under five years than any other single 'band'.

In July 1990 during the first appeal against a Disqualification Order under the CDD Act, Lord Justice Dillon suggested that as yet, guidelines had not been laid down and that fairness required a degree of similarity between the disqualification periods imposed by different judges or courts for similar offences, although it was emphasised that no two cases were the same and each should be decided on its own circumstances.

Under Section 4, the minimum disqualification period was two years and the maximum 15 years. Lord Justice Dillon suggested that this should be divided into three brackets:

1. The top bracket of over ten years should be reserved for particularly serious cases (e.g. a director who had been disqualified before).
2. The minimum bracket of two to five years should be applied where, although disqualification was mandatory, the case was relatively not very serious.

Table 5.1 Disqualification of Company Directors – Great Britain
Period of disqualification in years

	Total	up to 1 year	1 year to 2 years	2 years to 3 years	3 years to 4 years	4 years to 5 years	5 years to 10 years	10 years to 15 years
1987	159	6	12	31	10	50	40	10
1988	332	0	39	80	49	100	53	11
1989	303	6	36	91	39	64	58	9
1990	309	8	35	78	45	80	52	11
1991	263	1	37	62	30	75	49	9
1987 Q1	25	1	4	3	2	7	6	2
Q2	25	2	1	6	0	9	7	0
Q3	46	0	1	8	4	18	13	2
Q4	63	3	6	14	4	16	14	6
1988 Q1	63	0	8	15	11	16	9	4
Q2	66	0	9	13	11	23	9	1
Q3	96	0	13	18	13	34	14	4
Q4	107	0	9	34	14	27	21	2
1989 Q1	84	0	11	28	10	18	14	3
Q2	71	0	6	25	8	17	12	3
Q3	70	4	6	18	12	13	16	1
Q4	78	2	13	20	9	16	16	2
1990 Q1	96	3	13	19	19	25	13	4
Q2	91	2	8	29	9	27	14	2
Q3	63	1	8	18	6	10	16	4
Q4	59	2	6	12	11	18	9	1
1991 Q1	66	1	7	13	7	23	11	4
Q2	69	0	13	20	6	18	10	2
Q3	58	0	1	12	3	22	17	3
Q4	70	0	16	17	14	12	11	0

Source: DTI statistics. Reproduced with the permission of the Controller of Her Majesty's Stationery Office.

3. The middle bracket of six to ten years should apply to serious cases that did not merit the top bracket.

The wording of the relevant section of the Act is quite clear and states in plain ordinary English that the conduct of the director of the insolvent company was such as to make him

'Unfit to be concerned in the management of a company'. With these firmer guidelines on disqualification periods, it should be significantly easier to make the punishment fit the crime!

There is a school of thought that firmly believes that until the legislation to curb the 'unfitting conduct' of certain directors is strengthened far more substantially, perhaps even with custodial sentencing, there will always be company directors who will run the gauntlet of the CDD Act and the Insolvency Act.

Although it might prove to be an emotive deterrent, it could stretch our already straining prison service to the very limits — particularly if the number meriting more than a slapped wrist continues to rise with the number of corporate insolvencies!

I am quite sure that a far more suitable remedy would be to hit them hardest where it really hurts — in the pocket. By strengthening the compensatory aspects of the Insolvency Act so that there was a very real chance that erring directors would have to put their corporate hands into their own personal pockets, not only would it encourage drastically more responsible attitudes from directors, but would also lessen the financial burden on the creditors.

Directors' conduct

It is the liquidator's duty, amongst other things, to report to the Department of Trade and Industry on the conduct of directors of insolvent companies. He is an officer of the court as well as being an agent for the company. If the company is being wound-up through the courts, then the Official Receiver normally undertakes this duty. However, it is most important that any relevant facts and information are laid at their disposal, whether by a creditor or an employee or perhaps just a member of the public. After all, the success of the legislation can depend to a large degree on the effectiveness and judgement of the liquidator, and it is essential that he forms as realistic a picture as possible.

The DDA also includes within Section 15 the provision for a director to be made personally responsible for 'all the relevant debts of a company', if he is in contravention of a Disqualification Order or if he acts on the instructions of a person whom he knows to be the subject of a Disqualification Order, without leave of the relevant court to do so.

It is a Section that one presumes has rarely if ever been invoked and presumably serves to act as a deterrent to those who might consider side-stepping a Disqualification Order. But with the increasing numbers of failed companies and the number of disqualifications that have now been made, a creditor might consider it time well spent ensuring that the company directors of the debtor company he is concerned with and any advisers or shadow directors, do not fall foul of this section of the legislation.

A register of disqualified company directors is available for inspection at Companies House in London between the hours of 9 a.m. and 5 p.m. There is also a register at Companies House in Cardiff. The Insolvency Service also holds details of any disqualifications they have been concerned with, but this is generally for internal use and not available for public inspection.

THE 1986 INSOLVENCY ACT

If the Company Directors Disqualification Act was designed to act as both a deterrent and if necessary a means of retribution against erring company directors, then The Insolvency Act 1986 reinforces this but also tries to simplify the complex field of insolvency.

One way that it tries to do this is to provide a way for

insolvent companies either to find a possible re-structuring plan to survive, or to liquidate the company in the way best suited to all concerned. It introduced various new remedies that directors of insolvent companies might utilise either to wind-up their company, or perhaps nurture it through a difficult period with the help of a member of the newly-created profession of insolvency practitioners.

It has also been said that the legislation shifts the director's priorities away from just honesty and conscientiousness, to those of skill and diligence. Presumably, the latter two attributes are an addition rather than a substitution!

The Insolvency Act is a vast piece of work, not just considered in terms of its scope and implications — but in sheer mass! Compared with the DDA of some 16 pages, there are several hundred pages of closely printed text.

Groups of Parts

It is broadly divided into 'Groups of Parts', of which there are three. The First Group of Parts concerns insolvent companies and companies winding-up; the Second Group of Parts refers to individuals and the third group contains matters referring to both of the previous groups.

In the first group, parts one and two deal with Company Voluntary Arrangements and Administration Orders whilst part three deals with Receiverships, Receivers and Managers and the situation as applies only to Scotland.

Part four includes a lot more text and deals with the Winding-up of Companies. This takes us from the preliminary points of Chapter one, through the various types of procedures, the responsibilities of the liquidator, the dissolution of companies after the winding-up to the intriguing Chapter ten, which includes various sections concerned with malpractice during and in anticipation of a Winding-Up Order.

All these bright new ideas are very refreshing and certainly have their place in the scheme of implementing more suitable and effective insolvency laws, but from a creditor's point of view they do not necessarily offer a great deal of comfort.

However, Section 214 seems to toss a little glimmer of hope in the out-of-pocket creditor's direction, with the introduction of the term 'wrongful trading'.

With all its various sub-sections and conditions, it appears to offer an opportunity not only to encourage a diligent and responsible attitude from directors, but also the possibility of compensation for creditors of insolvent companies who suffer financial loss because the directors have not adequately fulfilled the expectations of this Act.

An application under Section 214 of the Insolvency Act can be made only by the liquidator. If it appears to him that a person who is or has been a director of an insolvent company knew or ought to have concluded prior to the commencement of the winding-up, that there was no reasonable prospect that the company would avoid going into insolvent liquidation, then Section 214 states that the court is able to declare that 'a person is to be liable to make such contribution (if any) to the company's assets as the court thinks proper'.

In plain English, Section 214 seems to say that if the directors of a company continued in business even after they knew — or should have known — that there was no prospect of avoiding insolvency, then those directors could be made to put their hands into their own pockets to compensate the company's creditors.

However, these principles are subject to a subsection — of course — that states that the court shall not make such a declaration if it is satisfied that once the director concluded the company could not avoid going into insolvent liquidation he took 'every step with a view to minimising the potential loss to the company's creditors ... he ought to have taken'.

The advice contained within this section for the court's or liquidator's guidance as to just how that director should have concluded that insolvency was inevitable and just what steps he should then have taken to minimise the potential loss to creditors, is somewhat alarmingly vague.

They suggest that the required conclusions and steps 'would be known or ascertained, or reached or taken, by a reasonably diligent person having both the general knowledge skill and experience that may reasonably be expected of a person carrying out the same functions as are carried out by that director in relation to the company and the general knowledge, skill and experience that that director has'.

Once again, it is largely a subjective matter, leaving much to the whim and discretion firstly of the insolvency practitioner or Official Receiver, who is required to report on the conduct of the company directors, and ultimately of the liquidator and the powers that be.

Presumably, the wording is intentionally less than specific, theoretically providing more scope for the courts to ensure that culprits are not easily able to slip through any loopholes; whether this is the case or whether the courts would be better served with firm guidelines still remains to be established at this time.

To understand just how the courts interpret this area of the legislation and the various points upon which they lay emphasis, it is useful to look in detail at the outcome of an action taken under Section 214 of the Insolvency Act.

Produce Marketing Co. – case study

One well documented example of a successful Section 214 Action is the case of Produce Marketing Co. (PMC), a fruit importation agent. First incorporated in June 1964, Mr Murphy and Mr David were the sole directors from July 1981. In 1980 there was no overdraft, assets exceeded liabilities and no significant trading loss. By 1984 there was a £91,758 overdraft and an excess of liabilities over assets of £58,592. PMC's credit facilities with its bankers, Banco Exterior SA were apparently secured by a debenture and by Mr David's personal guarantee for £30,000. Mr Murphy, an experienced book-keeper, prepared trial balances at roughly monthly intervals. Although not an accountant, he had the time and skill to keep a close eye on the overdraft position and any unpresented cheques.

There was a history of PMC's accounts being prepared and submitted late. In common with many other small companies, the directors acquiesced in accountancy delays.

By the summer of 1986, the company's position had deteriorated sharply. The bank overdraft agreed at £75,000 was quite frequently exceeded. Not only had the personal guarantees been left far behind, but PMC was living from hand to mouth. At 31st July 1986 the PMC ledgers showed a deficit of £167,739.

In August 1986 Mr David requested an extension of the £75,000 overdraft facility with an inaccurate and optimistic approach to the bank. It achieved the necessary result and the bank extended the facility until January 1987 on the same security as before. However the limit was constantly exceeded and the bank finally lost patience in November 1986 and began to return cheques unpaid.

In January draft accounts were submitted by the auditor for the years 1984/5 and 1985/6, showing a grim picture. For the first of the two years, the turnover was down and the year's loss was £55,817. With an adjustment for a prior year the excess of liabilities over assets was driven up to £132,870. Trade creditors were £85,004 and the overdraft was £95,546. By the following year, trade creditors had risen to £143,454 and the overdraft to £118,171.

The accountant phoned Mr David and voiced fears that the directors might be liable for fraudulent trading, which was followed by a letter. The directors were also sent copies of Section 213 (fraudulent trading) and 214 (wrongful trading) of the Insolvency Act 1986.

The accountant prepared a cash flow projection for presentation to the bank in support of an application for further extension of facilities. It showed anticipated receipts, supplied by the directors, which were at the top end of their expectations and were unrealistic.

In February 1987 there was an interview at the bank. The auditors accompanied the directors. Initially, the response from the bank was unfavourable, but it had a change of heart and called for a £5,000 reduction in facilities coupled with a further reduction of £5,000 in April and another in June.

At that stage Mr David said that he was aware PMC was struggling but the company continued to press on even with the tightening constraints of the reduction in bank facilities. During 1986/87 there was a slight reduction in the overdraft but this was largely because of an increased indebtedness to Ramona Limited, one of PMC's shippers and one of its largest unsecured creditors.

In August, at its bank's insistence, Ramona instructed their solicitors to investigate the state of trade between themselves and PMC. At the same time, the directors appreciated that PMC was in desperate straits and there was no prospect of Ramona being paid what it was owed by PMC. As Ramona refused to co-operate in a rescue proposal, PMC went into Creditors Voluntary Liquidation on October 2nd 1987.

In these proceedings, the liquidator sought a declaration under Section 214 of the Insolvency Act, that the directors should each contribute £107,946 to PMC's assets. The issue was seen as whether or not the directors 'knew or ought to have concluded' that there was no reasonable prospect that PMC would avoid going into insolvent liquidation.

PMC's accounting records were adequate for the purpose of its business but woefully late. Although the directors did not have the accounts in their hands until January 1987, they were aware that the previous trading year had been a very bad one. They had a rough idea in July 1986; although they did not have the precise figure they knew that it was well down on the previous year.

They ought to have concluded at the end of July 1986 that there was no reasonable prospect that PMC would avoid going into insolvent liquidation. They did not take every step to minimise the loss to creditors within Section 213/214 and continued to trade for another year.

The court's discretion arose under Section 214, which was compensatory rather than penal.

Prima facie the appropriate contribution was the amount by which the company's assets had been depleted by the directors' conduct, which caused the discretion to arise. But Parliament had chosen very wide words of discretion and it would be undesirable to seek to spell out limits.

Taking all of the facts into account, this was a case of failure to appreciate what should have been clear rather than a deliberate course of wrong-doing, but that there were occasions when positive untruths were stated and that the auditor's most solemn warning was effectively ignored, the court declared that the directors were jointly and severally liable to contribute £75,000 to the PMC assets.

Having looked at the Law Report of the above case, it is interesting to look at the attitude the court has taken concerning the amount of the compensatory award. It seems that this amount is a token award, rather than a carefully calculated figure to indicate just how much additional money creditors lost because the directors had continued trading once they had passed the point where they should have realised that their company could not avoid insolvency.

What does not seem so clear cut is the court's attitude to the behaviour and conduct of the two directors. The directors' 'failure to appreciate what should have been clear' is precisely one of the requirements for Section 214 to apply and should surely not serve as a reason for their responsibility as directors to be diminished? The Act serves to encourage higher standards and competence from those who wish to be officers of a company and should not be eroded by excuses of ignorance.

The section states that wrongful trading occurs when the directors continued to trade when they knew or should have known that it was not possible for the company to avoid insolvency. The fact that they had 'failed to appreciate' as opposed to following a 'deliberate course of wrong-doing' should surely have been irrelevant. They continued to trade when they should not have done and they did nothing to minimise the risk to their creditors.

Fairmont Tours Limited – case study

Another more recent case concerning Fairmont Tours Limited resulted in an award of £6,729 being made under Section 214, which appears to represent a precisely calculated amount. The case, which was heard in the County Court, was not widely reported and although the sums of money involved are not particularly large it does clearly illustrate the principle of wrongful trading.

Fairmont Tours Limited was a holiday company that went into Voluntary Liquidation on 6th July, 1988 with a deficiency of approximately £9,000. The company had traded for over three years with the accounts to February 1986 showing a loss of £232 and the figures to February 1987 showing a loss of £3,480. It had always had few assets, which meant that the reported losses resulted in an insolvent position. However, the company did not prepare projections or create proposals to improve the trading position and they also continued to accept deposits from customers.

It was calculated that debts of £6,729 had been incurred since the date the directors should have known that the company was insolvent and the court ruled that this amount was due from the directors to compensate creditors.

BANKRUPTCY – THE FACTS

Inevitably, the statistics for personal bankruptcy as well as corporate insolvency show a massive increase during the recent recession. These figures obviously reflect the great numbers of people who have been forced into bankruptcy because of the general economic climate as well as those hit directly by the vast numbers of business failures, such as traders without the protection of limited liability, that generally protects company directors from personal responsibility for corporate debt.

The Individual Voluntary Arrangement

The Bankruptcy Act 1914 and the 1952 Bankruptcy Rules have been enlarged upon by recent legislation. The Insolvency Act introduced a new procedure as a possible alternative to personal bankruptcy; broadly speaking, it is constructed along the same lines as the Corporate Voluntary Arrangements. The idea is that a debtor who is being pursued by his creditors can come to an arrangement with them for the payment of all or part of his debts over a period of time.

The debtor applies to the court for an Interim Order, stating that he intends to make a proposal to creditors and naming a qualified insolvency practitioner who will prepare it. This order prevents bankruptcy or other proceedings being taken by creditors for as long as the court thinks fit. The insolvency practitioner will call a meeting of the creditors and if 75 per cent in value of creditors attending the meeting approve the proposal, it will be binding on all creditors who were notified of it whether or not they attended. The arrangement is supervised by an insolvency practitioner. If it is made and honoured, the debtor will avoid bankruptcy and all the restrictions and associated publicity that go with it.

The DTI comments in its published notes *A Guide to Bankruptcy Law* that this form of arrangement particularly suits debtors who have friends or relatives who are prepared to add money to the debtor's assets, or debtors who have sufficient income to ensure regular sums are paid over to creditors. There are no formal limits concerning assets or debts and each case would be considered on its own merits.

The unpleasant alternative

If this type of arrangement works, it is vastly preferable to the alternative that unfortunately for many becomes unavoidable.

There is perhaps less of a stigma attached to personal bankruptcy now than ten or even five years ago. This is probably largely due to the fact that the recession has meant that most of us know at least one person who has been declared a bankrupt and many of them can be seen as tragic illustrations of a miserable economic climate. There have even been instances of a kind of 'inverted snobbery' amongst bankrupts, with boasts of who 'went down' for the largest sum!

The DTI notes describe bankruptcy as 'one way of dealing with the financial affairs of someone who cannot pay his or her debts (a debtor)'. The intention of bankruptcy proceedings are said to be two-fold:

1. To free the debtor from an overwhelming situation and enable him to make a fresh start.
2. To make sure that available resources are fairly distributed among those owed money (the creditors). This will be done by a trustee who may be the Official Receiver or a qualified insolvency practitioner.

An enquiry procedure requires the debtor to explain just how he came to be in debt, and may include an examination in court or possibly prosecution if the law has been broken.

If the debtor owes less than £20,000 and has assets worth at least £2,000, the court will refer the matter to an insolvency practitioner to see if a voluntary arrangement can be agreed with the creditors to avoid bankruptcy.

As with corporate insolvency, a creditor can only petition the court for a Bankruptcy Order if there is an unpaid debt of at least £750.

Once a debtor is made bankrupt, he will no longer have a direct responsibility to his individual creditors. With the exception of fines imposed by a court, creditors cannot expect preferential payments even if they have been actively pressing for money up to the time of the bankruptcy. Every single creditor is now involved, not just those previously seeking payments. This should have the effect of relieving the pressure that the bankrupt will have been under. For example, anyone supplying a service to the debtor's home such as electricity or gas is required to treat him as a new customer from the date of the order and cannot press for settlement of unpaid bills.

The debtor no longer has control of his assets, with the receiver or insolvency practitioner becoming trustee of the bankrupt's estate. Naturally, the costs of the bankruptcy are the first matters to be dealt with out of the assets.

The bankrupt is entitled to keep certain items such as tools, books and small items of equipment used personally by him in his employment or business. In exceptional circumstances vehicles necessary for work may also be retained. Clothing, bedding, furniture and household equipment 'necessary for satisfying the basic domestic needs of the bankrupt and his family' are also exempt. The trustee can also recover property if he believes it was disposed of in ways that were intended to disadvantage or defeat creditors.

A bankrupt is restricted in many ways including:

- being unable to obtain credit of £250 or more alone or jointly without disclosing his bankruptcy;
- being unable to do business in another name from that in which he was made bankrupt;
- being unable to be concerned in promoting, forming or managing a company without the court's permission.

There are also certain public offices that he is not able to hold.

After two years, if the debtor owes less than £20,000 and has not previously been declared bankrupt within the past 15 years, he will be discharged from bankruptcy. If these conditions are not applicable, it is a period of three years. This obviously depends on his having played the game and not broken any of the rules.

Caring legislation

The legislation seems to be trying generally to act in a caring manner towards the bankrupt and his family whilst still ensuring the best possible return for creditors. The DTI's own description of just what the proceedings are intended to do puts forward firstly the intention to 'free the debtor from an overwhelming situation and enable him to make a fresh start', whilst secondly ensuring that 'available resources are fairly distributed among those owed money'.

When compared to the aspects of the legislation that refer specifically to company directors as opposed to individuals, the emphasis seems to have been distinctly shifted. Once a company director is aware, or should have been aware, that his company is insolvent his first responsibility is to minimise the risk to his creditors. This obligation is contained within the 1986 Insolvency Act. It is a vast change in the priorities for directors who have previously always looked to the best interests of their company first.

Not ever having been declared bankrupt, or been owed money by a bankrupt, I cannot speak with first hand knowledge. But it does seem to me that the creditors run a poor second to the bankrupt himself and I know of a number of 'victims' — from both sides of the fence — who have expressed similar views.

However, there are punitive steps that can be taken against the rogue who believes that bankruptcy is an acceptable alternative to facing up to his financial responsibilities.

PARTNERSHIPS

This is an area of insolvency that distinctly needs clarification and more detail as there is little guidance contained in the Insolvency Act. Insolvency practitioners themselves vouch for the additional complications that often occur with such situations.

As with sole traders, the partners in a partnership have complete responsibility for all their financial commitments. It is like a marriage in that the bond is broken either by death or by dissolution, but it can also be broken if one partner becomes bankrupt.

If the partnership becomes insolvent, but the partners themselves are still solvent then the procedures are fairly straightforward and the law and procedure that applies to sole traders applies with the appropriate modifications.

The partners can jointly petition for the dissolution of the partnership, or a creditor can bring a petition. If there is a shortfall between the partnership's assets and the partnership's debts — which there must be effectively if it is insolvent — then the financial responsibility is immediately transferred to the individual partners.

If they are able to pay these sums immediately, then they will not necessarily also become the subject of insolvency proceedings. However, it is very common for partners also to be insolvent and petitions issued simultaneously against them individually and the partnership.

In due course, the partnership will be wound-up as an unregistered company under the Companies Act, at which point the partners are deemed to be directors or officers of the company for the purposes of the Insolvency Act and the DDA. They are also subject to the same responsibilities and the inherent liabilities as a director of a limited company.

The situation becomes far more complicated if not only the partnership is insolvent, but also one or perhaps all of the partners. There are then claims between creditors of the partnership and secondly, there are claims between creditors of a bankrupt partner and any solvent co-partners.

Generally speaking, if an order is made against the partners, all of whom are bankrupt, then the creditors can claim firstly against the partnership assets. If there is an unpaid balance outstanding after this, then these sums can be claimed from the partners. Should there be a surplus, then this would be divided between the partners according to the shares set out in any partnership agreement in existence.

There are some exceptions and additions to this rule of thumb, but the overall picture is very similar to that of individual bankruptcy procedure as it applies to the sole trader.

As a creditor of an insolvent partnership, appropriate advice at an early stage is generally essential. Often, the partners are also involved in other businesses, either protected by limited liability or as sole traders, and winding-up can become very complex.

The fact that a sole trader or partnership has no protection of limited liability can sometimes seem like an attractive enticement to do business on a credit basis. The prudent businessman, however, would be well advised to ensure that there are suitable uncharged assets available should insolvency follow. The old saying that 'You can't get blood out of a stone' could be very aptly applied to this type of situation!

As with the CDD Act, there are many facets of the Insolvency Act that merit examination and discussion, but from the point of view of the creditor, we have specifically examined certain areas that are of particular interest to creditors. But it is well worth making a visit to your local reference library, where you will find a copy of this Act — amongst all the others! A basic understanding and knowledge of this legislation can be so important to all of us in business today. As many have found to their detriment, the creditor of an insolvent company treads a very fine line between being a creditor and becoming insolvent himself.

It is not as difficult to understand a 'statutory instrument' as you might imagine. Once you have developed the necessary knack of ignoring the pomp and legalistic waffle, you should soon find yourself able to pick through the meatier bones of the legislation.

CHAPTER 6
Getting the law to work your way

In theory, the very existence of the new insolvency legislation should help to protect creditors by providing company directors with the incentive to act responsibly towards their creditors through the deterrent effect of possible disqualification or financial penalties when appropriate.

Having now taken a look at the actual insolvency legislation maze, just how can you, the creditor, ensure that it works in your best interests if you believe that a company director has fallen foul of the law?

The academic answer surely has to be that the law should not be used to further any one person's interests, it should be used in the pursuit of justice. There are many people, however, who will tell you that the Law and Justice can be two very separate entities! So instead, let us re-phrase that and simply try to see how best we can endeavour to see justice done.

Perhaps the most frustrating aspect of the recent legislation from the point of view of the creditor is that there is virtually no direct action that he can take against the directors of the insolvent company if he believes them to be unfit as directors, or that they have been wrongfully trading. Indeed, the very part of the legislation that could possibly be implemented to try and claw back cash from the directors personally, cannot be invoked by anyone other than the liquidator.

This can be made all the more frustrating when you consider that the insolvent company you are concerned with might not even have had a liquidator appointed at the present time — for example, if the company has an administrator or is in administrative receivership or is part of a current CVA scheme.

Should the liquidator decide that action under Section 214 is appropriate, then he will almost certainly seek financial under-writing by the creditors for any such action. One presumes the liquidator would only instigate such a course of action if he can see not only the likelihood of a successful outcome, but also that the directors in question have funds or assets to satisfy any order the court might make. (Here lies yet another obstacle, because the tracing and proof of ownership of privately-owned goods is a nightmare in its own right; ask any of the big banks or lending institutions and they will gloomily recount their own horror stories of abortive attempts to do so by private investigators, debt control specialists and even ex-policemen.)

DISQUALIFYING A DIRECTOR

Section 6 of the CDD Act, which deals with the disqualification of 'unfit directors' of insolvent companies, specifies that only the Secretary of State or the Official Receiver if instructed to, can initiate proceedings under this section. It suggests that aggrieved creditors should complain to the insolvency practitioner concerned, upon whom they can rely to report to the Secretary of State.

Arguably, Section 6 is the most 'broad based' of the grounds for disqualification and again it is a little frustrating that it is a 'closed shop'. More than 90 per cent of the disqualification actions taken by the Insolvency Service are taken under Section 6, according to a senior examiner in the disqualification unit.

It is also possible for a disqualification to be made under Section 10 which encompasses 'wrongful trading', but only where a declaration has been made under Section 213 or 214 of the Insolvency Act. In his book *Disqualification and Personal Liability of Directors*, L S Sealy is of the opinion that the wording of the Act seems to indicate that anyone interested in the litigation can ask the court for an order. However, my discussions with a senior examiner at the Insolvency Service show that they disagree with this. They suggest that it would be the liquidator who would 'draw the attention of the court' to such matters and it is purely a discretionary — and apparently virtually unused — power of the court.

An expensive business

Actions brought against directors under the CDD Act and the 1986 Insolvency Act can be expensive, obviously according to how vigorously they are defended and how complex the situation. According to a Senior Examiner within the Disqualification Unit of the Insolvency Service, their records indicate that costs for Disqualification Orders in 1991 ranged from between £100 and £2,435.55 per individual.

Although it initially appears frustrating that the creditor is not able to take any decisive steps towards having a director disqualified or to seek recompense under Section 214, it is worth giving serious consideration to the financial implications to which creditors could be leaving themselves open.

If it were possible for a creditor to seek to take action in such cases, the legal fees would likely be prohibitive. He would also face the constant frustration of continually finding that a great deal of relevant documentation concerning the insolvent company is unavailable for public inspection.

I firmly believe that once a company is insolvent and is being liquidated, then creditors or their representatives should have free and unencumbered access to all the company's records — not just the data store at Companies House — that could be considered pertinent to the insolvency and the trading of the company. In a free society, this access to information should be considered as a natural right, not a privilege allowed to a handful of professionals and those who could well be disadvantaged by the revealing of such information.

It seems reasonable to suggest, then, that the creditor who is seeking the disqualification of a company director has little recourse other than to provide the insolvency practitioner, the liquidator and the Insolvency Service at the DTI with as much relevant, factual information as possible — and leave the job to them.

COMPENSATION FOR CREDITORS UNDER SECTION 214

Likewise, as it is not possible for a creditor or anyone other than the liquidator to initiate an action under Section 214 that might eventually result in the director(s) being ordered to contribute personally to their company's assets, I believe it is, again, very important that you ensure that the officials dealing with the liquidation are made aware of any relevant facts.

You will almost certainly need to adopt a very positive 'I won't be ignored' attitude when dealing with any of the parties involved in the receivership and liquidation. It seems sad to say it, but unfortunately life in general tends to show that it is the more vociferous of complainants that are heard and noted — and I have no reason to believe that insolvency is any different.

If the only course of action is for you the creditor to provide information concerning the directors to the officials who are liquidating the company, at the very least you have a way of ensuring that your points are heard, noted and considered as part of the overall picture of the company director's behaviour. Firstly, though, decide whether or not you have a genuine grievance against the directors of an insolvent company. You must look impassionately at the facts and information that you have available. You have to overcome the primitive instinct that tells you simply that they owe you money: they have it — you want it!

If any action is to be taken against the directors by the liquidator under Section 214 of the Insolvency Act, or later under Section 10 of the CDD Act, then as discussed previously he must believe that the directors were aware that it was inevitable that the company would go into insolvent liquidation some time before the actual winding-up, and at the same time had failed to minimise the risks to creditors.

Whilst the liquidator — and you — will be considering whether this has happened, the director will be considering his best defence against any such accusations; whether to plead total ignorance of the impending insolvency, or to argue that he took those necessary though vague 'steps to minimise the loss to creditors'. He might insist that he 'stayed at the helm' of a potentially sinking ship specifically to try and minimise any such losses.

The liquidator, administrative receiver or administrator will have access to all the documentation and paperwork that you would probably give your right arm for a glimpse of! However, he should provide you with a great deal of background information in his report to creditors, which you should read and study very carefully. It will show the steps that led to the decision to appoint receivers, whatever the type of receivership, and will indicate to some degree the preceding actions of the directors.

It is possible that the report itself might indicate that the directors were given warnings of their situation, but chose to ignore or disregard them. I have seen a creditor's report that gave scant details — that is, confirmed the existence — of a report made on a company at the behest of its bankers some three or four months before those same bankers finally appointed an administrative receiver.

The report apparently gave clear indications that the company was already insolvent and that the directors 'should be mindful of the implications of Section 214 of the Insolvency Act'. However, almost two years after that report, and a further report by the insolvency practitioner handling the administrative receivership citing the directors for unfitting conduct, the DTI are still, I understand, 'seeking further information about the company'.

Meanwhile, the creditors have been unable to gain sight of the report provided to the bank; the bank has — under their fixed and floating charge and another further security of cross-guarantees on assets with other companies in the same group — made sure of their pound of flesh, which rose from £700,000 in September 1988 to £4.8m in June 1990; those same directors are still directors of up to a dozen or more other companies (most of whom bank with the same member of the 'Big Four' that instigated the administrative receivership) and the creditors have been told to expect nothing! The bank chose not to call in their cross-guarantees with other companies in the same group.

The wording of the Section 214 as contained within the Insolvency Act is quite clear in its intentions — it's only at a later point that you begin to realise it is not as straightforward as you first supposed.

Gathering information

When you have read the report, read it again, and again a day later. If you possess a practical brain as opposed to one trained in this specific field, you will need to do this several times before you can absorb the information it contains. Try to do this with an open and objective mind and avoid the tunnel vision that can spring from desperation. Make notes of any details contained in the report that you wish to query, whether it is because you do not understand them or because you consider them to be inaccurate or incorrect.

Although the insolvency practitioners concerned will probably be extremely busy and might be less than helpful when dealing with your queries, once a point has been raised it will by necessity eventually come to the attention of the liquidator when you provide copies of relevant correspondence to him.

Another source of information is Companies House, where the latest details filed on the company will be kept. This will also provide you with details of any legal charges over property and is therefore a good point from which to begin to form a background into the actual assets of the company, and any others within a group if it is part of a larger organisation. Bear in mind, though, that even if the company is complying with all the regulations concerning submission of accounts and other documentation, even the latest information held at Companies House is often out of date by more than a year.

Companies House will also tell you whether or not the directors are also directors of any other companies. This gives you some indication of just how hard a Disqualification Order might hit the directors concerned. If their business interests extend to some ten or twenty directorships — and believe me, this is not uncommon — then a Disqualification Order will mean considerably more than a minor inconvenience. It can sometimes be quite an eye-opener to see with just how many companies some directors are involved!

One small point: Companies House has notoriously busy telephone lines but they do also operate a 'Postal Search Service'. Details can be supplied either as photocopies of documents held, or as a microfiche copy. The latter is cheaper but as they are in effect miniature photographic negatives, you will need to have access to an illuminated magnifier in order to read them. There are also several reputable companies who can extract information from the records on your behalf — for a fee.

Checking at the Land Registry

It is also now possible to visit the Land Registry and there you can 'investigate title' — look at the details — of registered property. This will show you current ownership, any changes in ownership and any charges (mortgages) on the property. If any property owned by the company has changed hands, the details will be recorded at the Land Registry. You might detect a recent change in ownership of company property, which might be construed as working as a disadvantage to the creditors of the insolvent company and perhaps give an indication that not only were the directors continuing to trade whilst aware that insolvency was unavoidable, but also that they were most certainly not acting in a way to minimise the risk to creditors.

Before they are all dispersed across the industry, it could be worth trying to speak to as many of the company's employees as possible — particularly from the accounting section. In larger operations, it is not uncommon for some staff, particularly in the accounts department, to be employed on either a temporary or occasionally a permanent basis by the firm of insolvency practitioners.

Be careful to listen for facts and information that can be substantiated and not hearsay; remember, these people have probably lost wages, holiday pay and their livelihoods and could be tempted to try to 'get even'.

It might be advantageous to go back over any other transactions you might have had with the firm recently or in the past. Has there been any change in their trading pattern, their system or timing of payments? Have they recently changed or adjusted their terms and conditions of trading? If possible, speak to other people who may have been dealing with them too — perhaps they had also experienced difficulties over a period of time or a sudden change in methods of payment? Have any of their cheques been dishonoured recently or in the past? Do you have any correspondence with them that might give any indication as to their attitude to you as a creditor, or their own knowledge and understanding of their financial situation? For example, perhaps they have indicated an invalid complaint concerning your goods is the reason for a late payment. Hindsight might show that their lack of cash was the real reason and this certainly does not indicate that they 'took every step to minimise the loss to creditors'.

It is worthwhile keeping in touch with the insolvency practitioners concerned with the receivership/liquidation. They will probably be less than receptive most of the time as you will simply be an irritation, but make them keep scratching. They will be extremely busy and preoccupied with the business of sorting through the company's affairs as swiftly and as economically as can be done. Professionally, their duties and priorities are laid down; morally, I have no doubt that they also have a duty to help and answer any queries the creditors might have. At the end of the day however, they will be paid exactly what they ask for as fair payment for the work they have done, regardless of any shortfall creditors will suffer.

Again, remember the 'I won't be ignored' attitude, because it is possible for even the most diligent of people to overlook important background information. The insolvency practitioners will be working to a budget and will probably be deeply entrenched with a mass of paperwork, figures and reports. You may well be aware of relevant information from outside the company that he would have no way of knowing. The insolvency practitioner or liquidator will also be interested to hear of any assets, whether company ones or those of a director, of which he is not already aware.

If you do have any information that you consider to be pertinent to the receivership in general or the director's conduct in particular, send it to the Insolvency Service as well as to the insolvency practitioner. The Insolvency Service is a vast network of sections and divisions that seem to communicate with one another on occasion, but do not be surprised if you never manage to establish contact with the same person twice!

You may also consider it worthwhile contacting your local Member of Parliament — particularly if he happens to belong to the party in power. (In a run up to the general election, you will probably find whoever it is much more willing to listen!) The likely course of action for your MP will be to write to the Minister responsible if he considers you have been treated badly. Of course, this does not imply that the insolvent company directors have actually done wrong, as the MP will probably have only very scant knowledge of the insolvency legislation.

What it will do, though, is keep your corporate debtor very much on the top of the pile. There are thousands upon thousands of directors who have been investigated and are candidates for this legislation. Insolvency practitioners are duty bound to report back to the Insolvency Service on directors' conduct and each year many, many thousands of 'unfitting' reports are filed.

Obviously sheer administrative limitations — particularly in the depths of a recession that has aggravated a depressing situation — mean that only a certain number are going to be dealt with each year. At the present time I understand that the back-log is quite phenomenal.

Occasionally it might be worth considering sending copies of correspondence, particularly when querying the director's actions with the insolvency practitioners, to the directors themselves, inviting their own comments or explanations. Naturally, the chances of getting any response are very remote but it might just send a slight twinge through their buttocks and perhaps cost them a little sleep!

To summarise, if you are hopeful that a disqualification action will be brought against directors of an insolvent company, you should:

- ensure that every relevant shred of information is passed to either the liquidator, the Official Receiver or the Insolvency Service (or preferably all or both if they're involved);
- you should aim to keep the matter on the 'top of the pile' and at the front of everyone's mind;
- keep detailed notes and copies of correspondence — and never send original documentation, just photocopies.

The same principle applies with a Section 214 action; keep lobbying all concerned and provide the liquidator with as much detail as possible. Remember, as emphasised before it is necessary to show that they not only continued trading after they should have realised they were insolvent, but that they also failed to take reasonable steps to minimise the loss to creditors.

I have also been advised by more than one insolvency practitioner that one of the reasons that there are comparatively few actions recorded under Section 214 is because many directors choose to settle 'out of court' once the liquidator shows his hand. So don't be discouraged when people tell you that 214 is a little used piece of legislation — and believe me there will be plenty of them; its very existence has proved useful in many instances.

Should a declaration be made under Section 214 against a director, then it is also possible for a Disqualification Order to be made under Section 10 of the CDD Act. Although, apparently, this is a little used section — as, in fact is 214 itself — and to date no one other than a liquidator has brought to the court's attention such a declaration, opinion seems to be divided as to whether or not it is feasible for a creditor to try and invoke these discretionary powers and seek a Disqualification Order under Section 10 of the CDD Act. It apparently awaits a test case!

The keyword to coping with such a situation has got to be patience; nothing moves swiftly when the wheels of justice begin to turn, and there is little that you can do other than try to oil the cogs that turn the wheels. At the very least, I believe it can be therapeutic to be as conversant with the procedures as possible and to feel that at least you are aware of what is — or should be — happening. Whoever said 'ignorance is bliss' had obviously never been bumped for a large sum of money!

CHAPTER 7

Predicting companies which might go bust

Perhaps the most important lesson we should all learn from having lost out financially to an insolvent company is whether or not anything could have been done to avoid this situation in the first place — and, of course, how best to avoid it happening again. There is a lot of merit in the theory that 'prevention is better than cure', but in business terms it can be very difficult to take adequate preventative measures.

PREDICTING WHICH BUSINESS MIGHT GO BUST

Whether you have an established credit control section within your company or personally check out your potential customers — or fall somewhere in between these two extremes — you will be presented with the same dilemma: what is the most accurate and reliable source for information as to a company's credit worthiness and how can you predict if a business is going to go bust?

As we have already mentioned, credit risk analysis involves not just an assessment of ability to pay, but also of willingness to pay. This will be a purely personal judgement and brings into the normally business-like spectrum of credit control what has been termed intuition, experience — or a hunch. You should always try to make that assessment alongside the traditional checks, but not instead of them!

Short of polishing up the old crystal ball, most of us are forced to rely on more traditional methods, such as bank references and credit checks. However, there have been a number of serious research projects into predicting company failures, although most were concerned with large companies. When you consider that something like 90 per cent of the firms in this country can be categorised as 'small' (having less than 200 employees) some recent research that has been undertaken into the failure of small businesses should make riveting reading matter.

The September 1991 issue of the *Journal of the Institute of Credit Management* published an article by John Innes, Colin Aitken and Falconer Mitchell, describing their research into predicting small company failure. I do not pretend to be able to understand the immense detail and the specific criteria they used for this purpose [for example, 'The estimates of the logistic regression parameters measure the effect on the log-odds in favour of the nonfailure of a particular variable'] but they do suggest that from the company sample they used there were distinct characteristics that were common to many that had failed.

They used two lists, one for financial and one for non-financial factors in appraising likely company failures:

Non-financial factors:
1 Did a director leave the company in the current year?
2 Was there a noticeable lag in time between the company's year end and the date of submission to Companies House?
3 Was there a lag between the date of the audit report and the date of submission to Companies House?
4 Was there a secured loan on the company's assets?
5 Did the company receive a qualified audit report in the current year?

Financial factors

Comparison of:

1 Current assets/current liabilities
2 Current assets-stock/current liabilities
3 Net profit/total assets
4 Current assets/sales
5 Total debt/total sales

They also highlight other case studies, which have specifically pin-pointed areas such as under-capitalisation, poor financial control or managers with expertise in only one function such as engineering. (I wonder whether engineers would feel it timely to respond to that suggestion with the comment that there are too many boards in the manufacturing sector that are bereft of engineers and overflowing with accountants and other such professionals!)

It has been said that businesses thrive or fail on their ability to manage their cash-flow successfully. If you detect a customer slowly — or rapidly — deteriorating in the way it abides by your terms for payment, then take steps immediately to ensure that it does not worsen by withdrawing credit temporarily or permanently, or adjusting the amount of further credit you feel safe to allow.

CHECKING CREDIT WORTHINESS

If you have a substantial contract/order pending with a company you have not traded with before, or perhaps not to such a high financial risk level, it is not only prudent but necessary to take any measures available to check their stability and credit worthiness.

If you feel competent to analyse the figures that will be available from Companies House, then for a small fee you can obtain photocopies of these. Bear in mind that they are likely to date from at least one year ago, because of the somewhat lax legal requirements for filing company accounts in England. In a rapidly changing market and particularly in a recession these figures will often do little more than suggest how they were trading, not how they are.

Trade references are largely considered to be something of a joke; let's face it, potential customers are hardly likely to provide you with the name of a company they are not paying! However, they are an extremely popular method of securing a cheap, quick and easy reference. If a bank reference is also obtained, it is useful to consider the two replies together.

Bank references

Banks will make 'bank to bank' reference checks on your behalf if asked to do so, and interpretation of these is something of an art in itself. The usefulness and value of these can depend to some degree on how good a relationship you have with your own bank manager. You must consider that the other managers are going to try and paint as rosy a picture of their customer as possible without being unrealistic.

When making the initial enquiry, be as specific as possible about amounts and the time-scale involved; the more detail you can give to your bank the better. When the reply is received, go through it with your own branch manager and anyone else who is involved with your credit control. The terminology used can make a vast amount of difference as to how the reply should be interpreted – don't put too much faith in a company that only 'should prove good' for example.

In a rapidly shifting market, make regular checks – not just the one at the outset of business. Remember, the bank can only offer a reference in good faith on a customer from the information that they have to hand – which is purely based on their financial standing with that particular bank. This could, of course, be an inaccurate picture.

A more broad-based check can be made by any one of the hundreds of credit information services that are in business, offering anything from a simple credit check on a particular company, through to those that can provide a complete credit control service.

Unless you are aware of a firm that has been personally recommended to you, a good starting point is to contact the Institute of Credit Management. They have an active membership and are able to provide a list of their members along with some good general advice.

It is a good idea to study the literature of a number of different firms and to assess just what is available, and what exactly you require. Most of these companies have vast databases with information on thousands if not millions of companies — often world-wide. Their information is usually compiled from a variety of sources including Companies House, banks and status reports and often quite exclusive information from other clients and customers who are dealing with the company — a sort of computerised grape-vine, really.

It is possible to request information on one specific potential customer, or have an 'on-line' access via your computer terminal to their databases, giving information as and when you require it. You will be charged accordingly. The main disadvantage is that you generally purchase the information 'unseen' and there is no telling in advance whether or not the information is as detailed or up-to-date as you require.

INSURING AGAINST RISK

It is also possible to go a step further and obtain credit insurance, although this can be difficult to establish in certain industries and for companies with a turnover of less than one million pounds per annum. Insurance is usually taken for the total sales ledger, or for one group of companies perhaps within one trading division, rather than for one specific account, as insurance companies are dubious about this kind of selection.

Naturally, there are a number of high risk areas for which it is difficult to obtain cover — the construction industry for example. There will also be exclusions, such as government departments, nationalised industries and your own subsidiary companies.

The insurance company will, of course, be keen to tell you of the efficient and extensive service it can offer, with details of their methods of credit checking and how they can identify your 'high risk' customers. Do remember when you listen to this and are thankful that they have helped you to eliminate your highest risks that it is, of course, in their own interests to ensure that your customers are likely to pay up and they are only insuring against a low risk portfolio of clients. After all, they will have to put their hands into their corporate pocket if a customer becomes insolvent or continually defaults.

It is sometimes possible, via your bank or an agency, to join a scheme that allows smaller companies to obtain the benefit of this type of insurance. Most good brokers will provide information on this subject and The Association of British Insurers can also provide a list of insurers to contact concerning this and other types of arrangement.

Factoring

Another method of minimising your risk and increasing your cash-flow at the same time is factoring and invoice discounting. To put it quite simply, factoring is where a company effectively 'sells' its invoices to a factoring company, who pay anything from 80 per cent to 90 per cent of the invoice immediately. The balance is paid over, less an agreed service charge, when the full amount is received from the customer. Normally an interest charge at a rate similar to that charged for an overdraft by the main lending banks will also be made on the sum advanced.

Factoring firms will quickly also add that there is not normally an arrangement fee such as that charged by the banks, and there is no security as such — they are effectively regarding your invoice as their tangible security.

Many years ago it was considered that anyone who opted for factoring was short of cash and could even be construed as a 'credit risk' themselves. Now the practice has spread and has become far more acceptable. There are many companies offering a wide range of services.

The Association of British Factors and Discounters comprises twelve of the UK's largest factoring firms, representing over 90 per cent of the market for factoring and discounting services. They can provide you with a very useful *Guide to Factoring and Invoice Discounting*, which explains the various services available.

Basically, the theory is that factoring will improve the cash-flow of healthy, growing companies and allow the management more time to spend on other aspects of their business, at which they probably excel. It is an often heard complaint of bankers and accountants that businessmen tend to see themselves as salesmen and consider their job done once the goods are out of the factory. The sad reality is that the time to pop the corks is when the cash is in the bank, but most of us are averse to 'chasing' sums of money, whether large or small.

It is possible to simply settle for a service known as invoice discounting, when all you require is a boost for your cash-flow and little else. You are advanced a percentage of your invoice but you retain full control of your sales ledger and are responsible for chasing the late payers. But factors can provide a full credit control service by taking over the sales ledger and actually sending out the invoices. They can also advise on credit worthiness from their vast databases. This full service factoring can be offered with or without credit protection (non-recourse or recourse factoring).

Non-recourse and recourse factoring

Non-recourse factoring will provide you with 100 per cent credit cover against a bad debt loss, whereas recourse factoring does not. The latter tends to be used by those companies with a wide spread of customers, or those already in possession of credit insurance. Some factors make a 'first loss' charge — similar to an excess on a motor insurance policy.

By regarding your sales ledger as a virtually tangible asset, you can see your business in a different light. Factoring can boost your cash-flow on the basis of just what your business is doing at this moment, whereas bank overdrafts are generally set based on historical criteria. In a recent survey of clients by International Factors, 49 per cent said that enhancing cash-flow was the principal reason for using factoring, whilst a further — and growing — 25 per cent were motivated by the desire to have 100 per cent bad debt protection.

It is possible to utilise factoring whether you are a sole trader, a partnership or a limited company. The factor will be looking for an expanding business, possibly in the early stages of development or expansion. A good spread of debtors is a considerable asset as is sound management and of course a good product. There are inevitably sectors they are not keen to become involved with — the building industry once again being the foremost. They are also reluctant to trade with companies that have a high level of disputes or credit notes.

If you think that this type of operation might suit your business, then you have nothing to lose by discussing the available options with one or several of the companies that can offer such a wide range of services. Before you come to any firm conclusions, you will of course make comparisons of costs and assess exactly what annual outlay you are likely to incur. It is important at this stage to consider whether this service could result in a saving on staff costs or perhaps improve your overall credit control and functioning. You may feel that your staff can cope with your credit control and invoicing but you would like to improve your cash-flow. Whatever your needs, select a package to meet *them* and not to suit the factoring company.

There is one other risk that directors of companies could find themselves exposed to since the insolvency legislation of 1986 — that is the risk of an action being brought against them should their own company become insolvent. Although not numerous, there have been instances of directors being made to contribute personally to the assets of their company under Section 214 of the Insolvency Act — some to the tune of almost half-a-million pounds. It is now possible to effect insurance cover against such actions and you might consider that it is worth investigating what is available.

Although it might seem initially to indicate that by doing so you are already aware of potential problems, it is more likely to be recognised as a sensible precaution, particularly if you are not involved on a day-to-day basis with the business or are perhaps not too familiar with your co-directors.

CHAPTER 8

Preventing it happening again

In addition to the ways that we have already examined of cutting the level of risk you take in business, there are certain principles that every type of business can consider taking on board to try and minimise the chance of incurring a bad debt. Even the construction industry, which often ranks as the flag-ship of recession hit industries and accounts for a large share of all failed businesses, could benefit from a little more forethought.

MONEY IN THE BANK!

Once you have a product or a service ready to offer the market, you will have two main problems in life: one will be getting the business; the other will be getting paid for it! This will apply to your business whether you are a one-man painter and decorator, a multi-million-pound civil engineering contractor — or perhaps a supplier of micro-chips. Neither of these crucial aspects of business has ever been easy, but in difficult economic times, both can become a nightmare.

I do not intend to tell you how to successfully win business; there are numerous sources for this kind of information specialised for each sphere of commerce and industry. However, it is worth noting that in a short-lived recession, it is not unheard of for firms to submit quotations for little more than their own costs, simply to keep the cash-flow flowing and the jobs from going. Those tactics can ensure short-term survival, but the pound of flesh will eventually fall due and in a deeper recession these tactics inevitably contribute to the high number of business failures. When it comes to taking every conceivable step to try and ensure prompt payment, then there are some vital points to remember.

Whether embarking on a large or a small contract, detailed paperwork is vital. However precisely and amicably matters are discussed and agreed verbally at the outset, it is essential that every detail is committed to paper and copies held by all the relevant parties.

Now is the time to note exactly what the terms of payment are, how and when payment will be made and, if you consider it prudent, what penalties might be incurred if these terms are not adhered to. It is advisable [and probably another sad sign of the times] to ensure that all paperwork is precise and detailed enough to stand up in a court of law if it ever proves necessary. Whether it is an initial order, contract or a variation to the original proposals — get it in writing.

RETENTION OF TITLE

Generally speaking, once you have provided goods, title passes from you to your customer when you invoice them, whether or not that invoice has been paid. However, it is possible to include in your terms and conditions of trading a clause relating to ownership of goods called a 'Retention of Title'. It should be properly worded by a solicitor and state that ownership and title remains in the supplier until such time as all invoices are paid in full, and failing that goods should be given up on demand. It must cover all goods and be binding, and should incorporate an express right to enter premises and remove goods. Such clauses need to be reviewed and refined not infrequently, because the law applying to RoT is also constantly being refined, but one that is properly constructed can ensure a legally effective weapon against bad debts.

If you have already commenced trading with a customer and now decide to include an RoT, you must draw their attention to this alteration in your terms and conditions and ensure that you have proof that they were aware of the change. Their signature on the new terms should prove adequate.

The RoT should also be shown on your invoices. A large number of companies have their actual terms and conditions of trading printed on the reverse side of their invoices for this purpose. If you decide to do the same, ensure that your stationery is flimsy enough to show that there is printing on the other side. The courts will not uphold the requirement for a businessman to examine the flip side of every piece of paper that passes through his hands just in case something is printed there! But if it is clearly visible that there is something there, then he should be diligent enough to read it.

Should the customer later become insolvent, you have a right to reclaim any goods or supplies still in the debtor's possession that you have provided subject to an RoT. Of course, a lot of companies simply send in half-a-dozen very large gentlemen to re-claim goods that are unpaid for regardless of whether an RoT is involved or not! The RoT simply gives you the legal back-up and does ensure that the liquidator cannot sell your goods as part of the insolvent company's assets once he is aware of the RoT.

PROFICIENT PAPERWORK, PROFESSIONAL ADVICE

A large percentage of disputes for payments in the service industries and particularly within the construction industry, hinge on additional work that has been undertaken over and above what was originally agreed. If the original contract needs to be specific, then it is equally necessary to ensure that you are in possession of definitive paperwork for additional work.

If you are operating in an industry where it would be plausible to anticipate this type of situation arising on a frequent basis, then be prepared and have standard 'Variation/ addition to Contract' forms printed in duplicate and ready for issue. On a smaller scale, keep a standard duplicate book in your possession and simply write down what has been asked of you or your company and get the appropriate signature before undertaking the work.

Don't underestimate the value of professional advice or assistance when it comes to formating a standard contract for your own use. It can be simply constructed, perhaps simply a letter in duplicate to your customer or client, with each party signing both copies and retaining one for their files. It needs to cover all the relevant points concerning payments, additional works and any charges incurred for overdue payments should they prove necessary.

Professional, qualified advice is not purely the domain of big business. Depending on the field of business you are operating in there is often very relevant and specialised help on offer from freelance personnel. For instance, in the construction industry there are freelance surveyors who specialise in agreeing stage payments, additional costings and generally help with the smooth running of a contract. Equally useful can be the freelance quantity surveyor who will be able to price contract work either from drawings or bills of quantities. Try and inspect a previous job he has priced just to ensure that you are happy to work on his margins, and discuss with him in detail any 'grey' areas.

PERSONAL CONTACT

If you are engaged in a lengthy contract, then another

important point (which has been stressed before, but cannot be pushed too hard) is to ensure a good rapport between the two accounting departments from the outset — whether that simply means you or perhaps your credit controller and the client's payments clerk, or two entire accounting sections. If you alienate their key staff at the first payment stage, then by the end of the contract, you will probably find there is very little goodwill remaining. If money is tight at the time, you may just be the one they will make wait for payment that extra month or two.

Learning to bite one's lip is often a very hard lesson in life and for a businessman it can be crucial. At the end of the day a little tact and diplomacy can go a long way. Good working relationships can form a network of excellent contacts throughout your industry. This means you are usually in the know about up and coming projects and new business — and inevitably the grapevine is often the first to warn of an impending collapse. If you are approached in business by a company you have not traded with previously, it is quite possible that amongst your contacts there is one who will have worked with them before. What was their payments record like? If they were made regularly on a standard computerised payments system, this would seem to indicate a good liquidity. If it seems that they only pay out when they have received a payment themselves, then exercise caution as you would probably experience a knock-on effect should the man at the top go bust!

If you are aware that you are caught in this situation — and many people are — then keep your intelligence up to date; make sure that regular credit checks are made either through your bank or a credit agency (see relevant chapter).

Try not to let the payments accumulate with delays and excuses; the easiest way to ensure your cheque is not 'caught in the post' is to have it collected by hand if you are aware of a timewasting exercise. Sometimes it can be advantageous to request your bank to make a special clearance on a cheque you are dubious about. The bank usually makes a charge for this of around £10 but it does mean that you know — usually within 24 hours — whether or not that cheque will be cleared. However, exercise caution if you are relying on those funds as some banks will still not regard that cheque as 'cleared funds' despite the special clearance confirming that the cheque will be paid. Counter-staff will sometimes gladly inform you that 'special-ing' a cheque does not actually get the money into the account any quicker. But it does give you the peace of mind!

Perhaps the most important thing to remember is that if you're in business, you must accept the risks; there is no exact science to ensure successful credit control, no foolproof method of identifying potential bad payers.

Thanks to David Theobald for his valuable assistance with this chapter and his expert advice concerning credit control.

CHAPTER 9

Inside the bank manager's head

YOUR BANK – FRIEND OR FOE?

However well-qualified and expert a businessman may be in his own specific field, the future health or sometimes the very existence of his company is inevitably in the hands of outsiders at certain times. At a time when there is a temporary crisis this means accountants, management consultants or insolvency practitioners, who are entrusted with the role of guiding the company out of troubled waters. But far more often and to a greater degree, it means the company's bankers.

Deciding upon the most suitable source for professional advice can be crucial and yet is often a 'shot in the dark', with little more than personal recommendations to go by. Hardly surprising, then, that companies frequently find they have shot themselves in the foot! But at least changing professional advisors is a reasonably simple affair; changing banks mid-stream is not necessarily as easy.

The prudent businessman is well advised to ensure that his bankers have a genuine understanding of his business and its needs, and are the best placed to accompany him along the road to expansion and greater profitability. The best time to do this is before the business encounters problems, not during or after. With a strong company, or a well-researched and presented business plan, you should find the banks approachable and keen to listen to your needs. Once you have hit choppy waters, they are less likely to want to be the ones to toss out a reserve lifeline!

But inevitably, there will be many businesses that only discover they do not have the support they need from their bank when they are perhaps threatened with a potentially catastrophic financial situation caused by a bad debt from an insolvent company. If the loss is onerous and the bank sees its security diminishing, as can happen during a property slump, the knock-on effect can be very swift and far-reaching. Often, however, careful re-structuring and a tight financial plan will encourage confidence from your bank, or become part of a successful presentation to a prospective new bank.

BANKING ON A WINNER?

An often heard criticism of British banking today is the lack of real competition between the 'Big Four' and their overall similarities in the handling of and attitudes towards their business customers – particularly the more diminutive of the species!

However, although governed by broad policy guidelines and normally with a 'ceiling' for lending power, many banks differ not only from one group to another, but from one branch to another depending on the manager *in situ*. A recent study made by David Deakins and Ghulum Hassain of the University of Central England in Birmingham into 'Risk Assessment by Bank Managers', not only highlights this fact but also sheds some light on the priorities, problems and general criteria that bank managers take into account when making their assessments.

Their research was based on a start-up business plan for a real company that is actually now trading, but many of the observations can be applied equally well to an existing trading company that is seeking alternative bankers.

Assessing risk – a case study

The proposed business had the advantage of well-qualified proprietors who were in senior management positions in a large firm within the same overall sphere of business. They therefore had vast experience not only of their subject, but also of management. The new business was to be involved in using specialised IT applications within the construction industry, which in 1991 was at the sharp end of the recession. However, although it was recognised that this fact might colour the judgement of managers, the prime concern was to establish the criteria that remained constant whatever the state of the economy.

The proposition was 'Highly geared; seeking a £60,000 facility for 2 years compared to an equity stake from the proprietors of £30,000. However, this was balanced by having security available in the personal assets of the proprietors.' In all cases, the size of facility required was marginally outside the discretion of the manager although there is generally an ability for them to report on such a proposition to a regional office with their recommendation should they feel the proposition worth pursuing.

A detailed business plan had been formulated, which included CVs of clients, business strategy, cash-flow projections for four years after start-up (from £60,000 in the first year to £555,000 by year four) with assumptions behind the income projections, as well as general background information on their specific industry, the type of service they would provide and the relationships with other parties that might be involved in the business, including a Dutch company that had worked extensively in this same field on the continent.

The sample is described by the writers as being 'representative of different sizes of branches and different banks across the West Midlands'. The bank employee responsible for making lending decisions to small firms is in each case referred to as a manager for simplicity although at certain banks the role is accorded a different title.

The managers all received the business plan well before the interviews, most by two weeks beforehand. However, although some took the opportunity to ensure they were well-prepared for the meeting, it was apparent that a number had only looked 'the night before', which would obviously have excluded the chance of their gaining any specialised knowledge or information on the industry in general from elsewhere.

Despite the obvious importance and strength of the qualifications and career background of the proprietors, a number of managers immediately focused their questions on the financial information provided. Those that took this aspect as a priority were also 'preoccupied with the lack of projected balance sheets and profit and loss accounts'.

A number of managers were also concerned about the effect on the proprietors of the drop in standard of living that would be necessary as they would effectively be taking a 50 per cent drop in income. Graciously, those managers also conceded that it did represent a high level of commitment on their part!

Some of the managers were also concerned whether or not the proprietors would be able to work successfully together, and indeed whether they all needed to relinquish their full-time jobs at the outset of the venture. As each man was bringing a different skill to the business, it could have been detrimental to its success if the proprietors had been influenced by the 'Don't give up the day job' kind of comments raised.

The links with the Dutch company were probed by virtually all the managers. As it was possible that there could be future investment from this source, it quite naturally acted as a honeypot to the banking bees. The researchers considered that the business's viability and future success was not dependent on 'going Dutch', but only one manager agreed with them.

Another common denominator amongst the managers seems to be a lack of experience of dealing with customers in such a specialised high technology field. Several expressed a view that it was 'above their heads'. Equally, relatively few were keen to pursue the corporate strategy or business aims and objectives, although one would have expected these to have been important areas.

A number of managers also seemed to lay more emphasis on firm commitments of work, rather than the fee-earning potential and experience of the proprietors. They were also keen to be provided with more detail of the general expenses of the business. In fact, it was the detailed financial facts and projections that dominated virtually all the discussions.

At the end of the project, the researchers found – quite to their surprise – that there was an almost equal split between positive and negative reactions by the managers to the proposal, although one can see from their actual statistics that the degree of enthusiasm or the lack of it did vary quite considerably. The results did not surprise me at all as I have always found bankers to be an extraordinarily fickle bunch!

The very relevant, and interesting lessons that can be learned from the managers' comments and their reactions to the detailed proposal put to them, could be invaluable to the businessman seeking a bank with a positive approach either to enable him to commence trading with a new venture, or to try and re-finance his existing business. To summarise the cogent points:

1 *Be realistic in your proposals and expectations*
   Banks are inclined to give a disproportionate degree of importance to the ability to provide security for a start-up venture, whereas an existing business has the proprietor's experience and 'track record' to justify its future viability. If your track record needs breaking, anticipate the likelihood of a low-geared loan ratio by managers who are fully aware of the bank's need for low exposure to risk of bad debt – and the effect a 'mistake' in lending can have on their own personal careers.

2 *Do your homework on the bank and your sphere of business*
   Most bankers are – with the exception of their chosen subject of banking – generalists rather than specialists. If yours is a highly specialised sphere, then try and find a manager who has at least a modicum of knowledge,

111

understanding and experience of your field. The inevitable hunch and manager's rule-of-thumb experiences in the past can come into play at decision making time, no matter how hard the banks try to eradicate it and if your type of business is known to him he will often colour his decisions accordingly.

3 *Do your homework on the financial details of your proposal*
By virtue of their training, their job description, and the very air they breathe — bankers understand finance, the management of money. If they are guilty of tunnel vision at all, then your sentence is to provide them with as much accurate and detailed financial information relating to your business as can humanly be expected. If you do not feel capable of supplying a top-notch portfolio on your company, then employ a consultant (if that is financially feasible).

THE HAND THAT PULLS THE PLUG

We have all seen and heard of business collapses that were triggered by the company's bankers, who appear to wade in regardless as soon as they see their security threatened. This is of course not always the case and I, for one, can quote from personal experience a classic example of exactly the opposite happening.

Timing the appointment of an administrative receiver – case study

A major bank finally appointed an administrative receiver some three months after it was initially made aware of the company's imminent insolvency by a report the bank itself had commissioned. During those three months, the company continued to take credit from suppliers – whilst waiting for a large and long-awaited stage payment from a third party, which one presumed reduced its bank borrowing –

before the bank finally drew the line. Those extra three months probably cost creditors hundreds of thousands of pounds in additional bad debts, all of which could have been avoided had the bank acted sooner. Admittedly, hindsight can be a very precise science, but surely the bank had enough information at its finger tips to see that there was no chance of avoiding insolvency?

Perhaps the most frustrating aspect of such incidents is that the Banking Ombudsman is not empowered to investigate any complaints unless they are between a bank and its customer. It seems that the only possible course of action if you are dissatisfied with the conduct of a bank that you do not personally bank with, is litigation. One can always hope that the insolvency practitioners now handling the receivership will also look into the bank's conduct in this affair in a circumspect and unbiased manner — particularly since the firm that carried out the initial report on the impending insolvency is part of the same group as the insolvency practitioners.

Do the banks have too much power?

A senior official from within the DTI's investigations unit agrees that the powers the banks can weald by determining whether to send in receivers either sooner or later merits serious examination. Whether or not legislation is required, or even desired, is something that would need careful consideration, but if one creditor — particularly a secured or preferential one — has knowledge of a company's potential or imminent insolvency by virtue of the fact that it is exclusively able to explore the accounts and paperwork of that company, then they should be bound to act in a manner that would 'minimise the risk to creditors', to paraphrase the wrongful trading clause from the Insolvency Act. This would mean minimising the risk to all creditors, not just themselves, and would place the same burden of care on them as is placed by law on the company when insolvency cannot be avoided.

Equally, the whole concept of an 'open-ended charge' being allowed to banks on company assets severely disadvantages other unsecured creditors, because they are only aware of the borrowing as at the last audited accounts. Who knows, apart from the directors and their bankers, how much that borrowing has increased since that time, and − equally worrying − by how much the assets have devalued or perhaps been over-estimated in the accounts?

It could be that legislation is the only way that the power held by the major banks is ever going to be seriously challenged. Theoretically, certain cases could indicate that there has been unfair preference shown to the company's bank prior to insolvency − but what liquidator is going to take on the full might and force of one of the Big Four?

It is impossible to generalise about just when a bank will decide that enough is enough. Every bank manager will tell you that each case is considered separately and that it is very rare for the bank to 'spring' a decision on the directors; there will inevitably be a period − however short − of discussions between the directors and their bankers, when it will become clear that time is running short.

A look at the published figures for administrative receivership appointments by debenture holders − the banks − does not say too much on its own, except that there are, sadly, a lot of them made. However, if we compare these figures extracted by Touche Ross from the London and Edinburgh *Gazettes*, with figures on the outstanding advances provided by Warburgs, we have something of a yardstick to measure them by. The table below shows comparisons for the month of May 1991 between the major banks' share of lending and their share of administrative receivership appointments.

Table 9.1

Bank	% Total UK Advances May 1992	% Admin Rec. Appt May 1992	% Admin. Rel. Appt Y.T.D.*
Bank of Scotland	6.48	2.92	3.89
Barclays	20.8	19.53	18.8
Lloyds	11.09	14.86	9.73
Midland	10.06	12.54	12.09
Natwest	21.02	18.37	21.83
Royal Bank of Scotland	6.52	4.96	9.42
TSB	6.7	.87	1.09

* Year to Date

Source: Percentages prepared from Touche Ross Administrative Receivership appointments by debenture holders for May, 1992 and extract from Warburgs' statistics on Sterling Assets showing outstanding advances for May 1992. Reproduced with the permission of Her Majesty's Stationery Office.

It would be unwise to attach too much importance to these figures, since we are not aware in this case of the spread of lending between large and smaller businesses, which could be particularly significant because administrative receiverships – like Administration Orders – tend to be more commonly used in seeking remedies for larger companies. But it is interesting to note that several banks are appointing administrative receivers in proportionately higher numbers than one might expect from their lending figures.

It should go without saying that maintaining regular contact with your bankers and providing them with as much up-to-date background and financial information as possible is always advisable, but at critical times of trading it is essential. If it is 'the hand that rocks the cradle that rules the world' then most certainly it is the hand that pulls the plug that rules the business!

CHAPTER 10

Providing a fairer deal for the creditor

Having taken a look at the new legislation and contemplated its implementation in terms of the frustrated creditor, perhaps an even more important step is to examine the ways in which the spirit of this legislation could possibly be furthered, improved and enhanced — if at all — and theoretically provide a fairer deal for the creditor.

STRENGTHENING THE CREDITOR'S HAND

There are those who will say that this legislation does not go far enough to strengthen the creditor's hand. Parts of the legislation seem to virtually 'privatise' the field of insolvency and perhaps effectively provide profit as part of the incentive and an assurance of responsible action. But it has also been observed that the element of protection afforded to creditors in the legislation could be greatly strengthened if the banks did not hold such a strong hand.

When they are afforded a fixed and floating charge by a company, they are taking very little risk, whereas other creditors, who are often unaware of the extent of current borrowing secured by such a charge, can be shouldering a heavy burden. As soon as the bank sees its own security either reached in borrowing terms or perhaps diminishing in value, it is free to 'pull the plug' not only on the company, but quite likely indirectly on a number of that company's creditors.

Under circumstances such as these, creditors are denied the knowledge and flexibility afforded to the bank. As Harry Rajak (Director of the Insolvency Research Unit at Kings College, London) recently observed, creditors can find themselves playing on a severely tilted playing field. If this were to be changed, then a major examination and rethink on banking procedures would be required, and most experts see this as impossible. They cite the fact that it could jeopardise the entire lending system — but perhaps that system is ripe for change.

Maybe the flexibility of the floating charge should be weighed more closely against the shrouding effect it has on a company's credit status. If a company's borrowing increases dramatically during the period between the filing of annual accounts at Companies House, and this is secured by a fixed and floating charge, the unsecured creditor has no way of determining whether a customer is in fact teetering on insolvency.

To be fair, the banks often find themselves in a 'no-win' situation, being criticised for lending too freely in the boom times and only too ready to pull the plug during the harder years. At the end of the day they are in business too, however, and the ground-rules they play to are often governed by the relationship you have with your individual manager. I have dealt with many different banks and many different managers in recent years and their attitudes have all been widely differing — from branch to branch let alone from bank to bank.

EDUCATING AND MAKE THE PUBLIC AWARE

In the broadest of terms, the greatest service that can be done to further the very high principles behind the Insolvency Act and the DDA is to increase public enlightenment and awareness. How can the law be a deterrent if the public is not aware of its existence? I hope that these pages may have increased public awareness in however small a fashion, but in general terms those who are not normally affected by, or specifically involved with, insolvency have very little knowledge of the subject.

The real broadening of knowledge must come from within the sphere of education and training itself, whether this is achieved by on-the-job, in-house methods, or greater exposure of the subject during business study courses for students. More emphasis and a sense of importance must be given to the understanding of the insolvency legislation and its value, therefore encouraging higher standards in the future managers of British commerce and industry.

The media must be kept informed of the successes as well as the shortfalls of insolvency legislation, and not left simply to muddle through with the odd 'sensationalised' article. The media have been cited many times for concentrating on bad news rather than good and likewise often seem to relish reporting failure rather than success; all too often, the only time this legislation is mentioned by the press is when they pick up a story that seems to illustrate another failing of the law.

A recent example showed a director as having purchased assets from his insolvent company to start up afresh; at first glance this appeared to highlight the ineffectiveness of the legislation to stop directors shirking their responsibilities and showed them actually profiting from their creditors' misfortunes. But it actually omitted to point out that a good and fair price for the assets was achieved by the liquidator to help satisfy creditors, and that virtually the entire work-force was taken across to the new company, along with most of the suppliers, who made arrangements with the new company enabling them to charge inflated or enhanced prices until the old debt has been settled.

However, a number of insolvency practitioners will tell you that they often see the same faces time after time at creditors' meetings, and there is a definite need for caution when dealing with a company that has risen phoenix-like from the ashes of its predecessor.

MAKING THE LEGISLATION MORE PLAUSIBLE

It must be considered that company directors are to some extent becoming more aware of the implications of the legislation, although the proportionately few numbers of disqualifications and actions under Section 214 will naturally encourage many to continue to run the gauntlet.

Insurance is now available to directors to protect them from the financial hardships the legislation could bring. Why not, then, call for a mandatory insurance for directors so that creditors can be assured of funding for an action under Section 214 and an actual cash payment if it is successful? It might also provide a further deterrent to erstwhile directors if they knew that their mandatory insurance premium would be sky-high if they were subject to a Disqualification Order or a 214 action — in the same way that drunk-drivers are penalised by their insurers once they regain their driving licence. Perhaps Employers and Public liability policies could be extended or complemented to include such a feature? There seems little point in having a piece of legislation on the statutes that is little used because of the financial implications and uncertainties of any actions brought under it.

Consideration could also be given to whether some of the vagueries of the Insolvency Act — and particularly Section 214 — should be eliminated with some tightening-up. For example, perhaps there should be criteria to be met by all directors. In 214, for instance, there could be a a *minimum* requirement set to show that the director had taken every step to minimise the risk to creditors. This would still allow the court the discretion of deciding that although the minimum was complied with, the true spirit of the law was brushed aside.

FREEDOM OF INFORMATION

If the legislation can be interpreted to provide for 'interested parties' to be allowed under certain circumstances to instigate a disqualification action under the CDD Act, then they should not be prevented from seeing all of the relevant paperwork of the company — possibly the very documentation that could show the true nature of the director's conduct. For example, with the possible culpability of shadow directors a fact, and bankers potentially falling within that category, how else can creditors be reassured that no stone has been left unturned, when it is quite possible that the person rolling those stones over was appointed by the bank in the first place?

If a company is heading for liquidation, this means that very soon it will cease to exist; so who benefits then from the on-going process of 'privileged and confidential' data — certainly not the creditor or the shareholders.

INSOLVENCY'S POVERTY TRAP

In addition to these points, I also feel that if the legislation is to work fairly for companies and creditors however large or small, then a further course of action in winding-up an insolvent company is necessary. As previously mentioned, for the smaller company that is virtually free of any assets, there is little option if it is insolvent but to apply to the court for a Compulsory Winding-up Order. Although it could be said that the directors have acted responsibly in taking this course of action, the same stigma is attached to it as if the petition was brought by a creditor. But the court and the Official Receiver are virtually the smaller businessman's only option if he has no funds, since most other routes will involve the services of an insolvency practitioner, who will normally only take on a case when he can see his own fees will be covered by the company's assets or from another guaranteed source.

At present, directors have no choice under such circumstances and their cases are perhaps not always handled with such tact and patient efficiency as those liquidated by insolvency practitioners. By virtue of the very job, the Official Receiver's Office is known to have a rapid succession of staff, who are unlikely to spend a great length of time developing their skills at this end of the insolvency scale.

If directors of an insolvent company with few or no assets petition for a winding-up order, perhaps the receivership and subsequent liquidation could be referred to one of a panel of insolvency practitioners, who would undertake to handle a certain number of company insolvencies despite an absence of company funds or assets. This could be funded either by a central fund organised by the profession, or perhaps from a mandatory insurance levy on company directors.

We have several back-up systems in this country to ensure that poverty does not preclude a person from getting the necessary help they require — legal aid and the NHS for example. Perhaps insolvency should now be considered on a par with these — it is probably one of the fastest growing businesses during times of recession after all!

Likewise, it has been said that the prohibitive legal costs in pursuing any action under Section 214 of the Insolvency Act have acted as a deterrent to creditors, as the liquidator will invariably look to them for the costs should he decide to instigate a legal action.

Contingency fees

I have discussed with a number of people, including an examiner at the Insolvency Service, the advantages of contingency fees for lawyers in such cases. This is, in a nutshell, where a lawyer will only take a fee — either agreed in advance, a percentage of the award or a combination of the two — if the case is won. It is common practice in a number of the states of America, but until recently has been resisted in this country.

The Lord Chancellor's department has produced a paper on contingency fees and it seems possible that a limited implementation could be on the horizon for this country. The government has indicated that it is looking favourably on removing the restrictions that now prohibit such terms, and that it sees the onus on those who do not wish to see the restrictions lifted to justify their case.

The examples set in the USA of huge damages awards and 'hounding' of victims by lawyers hungry for business have been cited as grounds for resisting the introduction of contingency fees in the UK. However, although a jury returns a verdict on damages cases in this country, unlike in the USA it is almost always the Judge who sets the amount of the award. He would of course be governed by strict criteria and guidelines as to the level of the awards.

If we are concerned about the impact these changes might have upon the conduct of lawyers, then surely we have little faith in our officers of the court? The suspicion that a lawyer might provide a client with biased advice in order to coax an early settlement could easily exist in the present system as well. Heavy work-loads have always put pressure on lawyers to 'tie-up' the less profitable cases quickly — but serious complaints on this score are relatively few.

The only real potential difficulty I can see is the 'nuisance' case, where less scrupulous individuals might try to bring malicious and unfounded actions against companies, in the hope of receiving an out of court settlement to save the company from bad publicity and to protect the good name and business of the company. It is worrying that should this happen, the businessman's costs could eventually be passed on to the consumer, who would pay higher prices as a result of litigation or threatened litigation, or the companies' increased costs from insuring against such practice.

However, if it is made clear that should an action be lost then the defendant's costs would have to be borne by the plaintiff, this should act as a suitable deterrent to such speculators!

A NEED FOR A NEW TYPE OF INCORPORATION?

The sweeping effect of the insolvency laws, which apply to all companies regardless of the size or nature of the business, might need to be adjusted if the Forum of Private Business is successful in its campaign to radically change the limited format available at present to create companies.

There are roughly three alternatives for the aspiring entrepreneur launching a new venture in this country:

- sole trader;
- partnership;
- limited liability.

Many small businesses, in particular, are established without limited liability. The laws governing sole traders and partnerships date back to the previous century and lay a great onus of personal responsibility on the businessman. Without the protection of limited liability, particularly in partnerships that falter, there can be a heavy financial burden.

But the structuring of the legal requirements for companies that have limited liability is the same whether that company

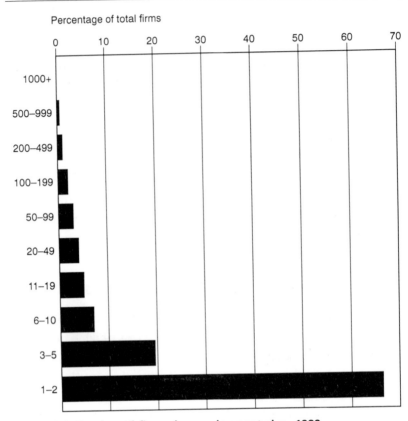

Percentage of total firms

Figure 10.1 Number of firms, by employment size, 1989

Source: 'How many small firms?' Michael Daly and Andrew McCann, *Employment Gazette*, February 1992. Reproduced with the permission of the Controller of Her Majesty's Stationery Office.

employs ten people or ten thousand! Whatever the format chosen, it seems that there is nothing specifically geared to suit the rapidly expanding numbers of small businesses. Even in times of recession, there are still thousands of people prepared to take the risk of starting a business. As Figures 10.1 and 10.2 show, they account for an enormous proportion of the number of firms in the UK, and are major employers in the work-place.

Percentage of total employment

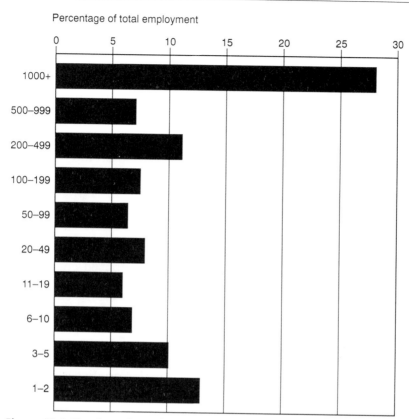

Figure 10.2 **Number of employed, by employment size, 1989**

Source: 'How many small firms?' Michael Daly and Andrew McCann, *Employment Gazette*, February 1992. Reproduced with the permission of the Controller of Her Majesty's Stationery Office.

The Forum of Private Business

The Forum of Private Business (FPB) is an organisation with over 18,000 members, which actively promotes free enterprise. They make full use of their members' comments, determining their policy by referendum and surveying members on a variety of subjects.

They are calling for a new and more appropriate legal format for small businesses, believing that whilst the small business community has undergone a transformation, their options for legal formats of business have remained outdated and are more appropriate to big business.

Their proposal is for the creation of an optional format called the 'Incorporated Business Firm', which would provide a sensible compromise between the largely unprotected status of sole tradership and the more complex obligations of a limited company.

Proposals were put to the FPB membership and the features that were supported include:

- simpler presentation of accounts;
- simpler constitutional documentation;
- clearer definition of director's duties;
- choice of tax regimes — partnership of limited company.

Whether or not the Forum has struck precisely the right, workable note remains to be fully examined. What they have rightly highlighted is the yawning hole in the current business legal structures.

A new form of incorporation could be applied to small, owner-managed businesses, and to those with only a small paid-up share capital. A simpler system of presenting the company accounts would help to ensure prompt submission and might even make them comprehensible to the layman!

A degree of protection of limited liability could be afforded, but balanced with a degree of personal liability for unsecured debts. In any event, small businessmen often find that their largest creditor is their bank and it is rare to find a bank offering credit without substantial security.

Whether or not a new form of business incorporation is established, it is worth considering that if all directors were personally liable to some form of legal obligation for a percentage of unsecured debts — in priority to secured and preferential creditors — the entire knock-on effect when a company fails could be reduced significantly.

BANKING ON FAIR PLAY

Comment has been made by various experts in the field of insolvency that the new laws have introduced a quite revolutionary concept. By stating that once directors realise that their company is insolvent, they must take all the necessary steps to minimise the risk to creditors, the emphasis of the director's prime responsibility is changed from the well-being of his own company to that of the creditor. It is quite a monumentous shift of duty for the directors and begs a conscientious reaction from them in respect of the creditors, who will be left behind once a company — in all probability — has ceased to exist.

Is it not time, then, for the financial institutions involved with insolvent companies to adopt a similar attitude to fellow creditors? After all, as advisors of the company they could potentially be construed as 'shadow directors', with all the implications that can bring. The banks seem so often to be unable to see beyond the end of their own noses when they take decisions concerning their own very well secured loans.

Whilst so many of them seem to conduct business as if they have three gold balls hanging outside the door, there is little hope for the small business, hanging by a thread at the end of the list of unsecured creditors. True, many entrepreneurs enjoy the stimulation of taking a calculated risk in business — the problem so often is that the money-lenders had marked the cards long ago and are invariably left holding at least five aces.

GLOSSARY AND SUMMARY OF TERMS USED

There are a number of characters who appear on the insolvency stage at various times and in differing types of insolvencies.

Administrative Receiver
This is an insolvency practitioner who has been appointed by someone holding a charge over all or most of a company's assets. He appears in cases of administrative receivership

Official Receiver
An officer of the court, he deals with compulsory liquidations amongst other things. He only becomes involved if the company is being wound-up through the courts and his duty is two-fold: firstly, to realise company assets to satisfy creditors and secondly to investigate the affairs of the company and report to the Department of Trade and Industry Insolvency Service.

Receiver
This is a person — usually an insolvency practitioner — who is appointed under the Law of Property Act 1925 by a secured creditor to receive income from, or sell assets, and his purpose is to discharge that creditor. Although the receiver has control of the company overall, the directors can continue to trade if the receiver considers it plausible. A company liquidation, then, does not always necessarily follow the appointment of a receiver.

Liquidator
A liquidator is an insolvency practitioner who is appointed to wind-up a company. A liquidator can only be appointed if the company has ceased trading and is being wound-up. In effect, he is an agent for the company and takes total control. There are various criteria concerning just who can take an active part in appointing the liquidator and exactly who he is, depending on the method of receivership employed.

Secured creditor

Often a bank or other financial institution with a mortgage or charge over company property, commonly referred to as a 'debenture holder'. They take the first and often only bite of the apple.

Preferential creditor

He has priority when a liquidator or administrative receiver distributes any company funds. There is a specific definition contained within the 1986 Insolvency Act as to in just what order these preferential creditors can expect their claims to be met and include VAT six months prior to the insolvency, Inland Revenue for PAYE/SC60/NIC twelve months prior, employees' arrears of wages and holiday pay together with some more obscure duties and EEC debts.

Unsecured creditor

Technically defined as a creditor whose claim has no secured prior rights, it means that you are near the bottom of the list along with all the other unsecured creditors. You will not be given any priority over the rest of the unsecured creditors whether yours happens to be the largest debt the smallest debt or the most interesting debt.

Shareholders

They come in last in the running order for picking the corporate bones.

Having looked at some of the cast of characters, we can now take a look at the different plots. There are fundamentally four different ways to say goodbye to a company, although inevitably there are various 'sub-sections' within each type.

1 Administration Order

This method is designed to be a constructive way of trying to save a company's business, or a way of securing the company's assets to enable an orderly winding-down of the company. It offers the company protection against the appointment of a receiver, who might not be able to realise such good figures for disposal of assets. The administrator — who will be a licensed insolvency practitioner appointed by the court — is there to protect the assets and manage the business while he prepares a plan of action to be included in a proposal to creditors. The plan will either suggest ways that the company could be more effectively organised and operated, or the most beneficial scheme to realise the company's assets.

This method has often been used as a rehabilitation process for troubled companies and was instigated to complement the procedures of receivership. In the past, companies that were still viable, but were badly in need of financial restructuring, had gone to the wall because there was no alternative.

The problems with this method are that it can be very expensive and in practice is used mainly by the larger companies. It can also be a lengthy process getting an administrator appointed, as petitions have to be drafted and served, whereas a receiver or administrative receiver can be appointed almost immediately.

In cases of administration, the creditor has very little influence over the final outcome; use your voting power here wisely.

2 Administrative receivership

This procedure is instigated by a debenture holder — that is, someone, usually a bank, who has a charge on company property. They will often have commissioned and received a report that indicates their security is at risk and will then appoint an administrative receiver to secure its monies. The administrative receiver will of course be an insolvency practitioner. Prior to any liquidation which may or may not follow, he will be responsible primarily to the body by whom he was appointed and *not* the creditors in general.

There is no precise criteria for why and when a debenture holder will appoint an administrative receiver; there are no rules or guidelines to curtail the debenture holders' power. However, administrative receivership does not necessarily mean that liquidation will follow — although it usually does in due course. There have been cases of companies being re-financed by a different bank and then continuing to trade successfully.

Again, the format of this type of receivership leaves the creditor with little sway; your voting power is your only chance of raising your voice.

3 Company Voluntary Arrangements

This was designed to provide a cheaper and less formal method of coping with a company's problems and the creditors are able to work towards a satisfactory conclusion with the insolvency practitioner handling the arrangement. It does not always result in a liquidation or winding-up of the company.

In such instances, the creditor must consider very carefully at the beginning whether they really believe that what often amounts to a 'stay of execution' is really the best course of action. CVAs need to be accepted by the majority of creditors, so it is quite possible for a scheme to be rejected.

4 Winding-up

There are three main areas in the field of winding-up, or liquidation as it is often called.

Members voluntary winding-up or liquidation

This occurs when the company concerned is solvent but wishes to cease trading. It often refers to a company formed with a limited purpose in mind — perhaps to raise funds to purchase a piece of medical equipment for the local hospital. Once that purpose has been satisfied with the necessary purchase of equipment, there is no further reason for the company to exist. A liquidator is appointed by the shareholders to realise the assets and settle all company debts in full within twelve months.

Creditors voluntary winding-up

This situation comes about when the directors consider the company's financial situation at a board meeting and a resolution is made that the company is insolvent and should accordingly be wound-up. Insolvency practitioners are then instructed to convene meetings at which a liquidator can be appointed.

This procedure allows the creditor far more of an opportunity to influence the final outcome of the liquidation. The appointment of the liquidator is crucial and although initially the members — directors — appoint a liquidator, this has to be ratified at the subsequent creditors' meeting. It is possible to reject their choice of liquidator and nominate an alternative.

Compulsory winding-up or liquidation

This is the winding-up of a company after a petition to the court. It is usually instigated by a petitioning creditor with a debt of £750 or more. However, directors can also petition for the winding-up of their own company. This may well occur when there are few or no company assets, because insolvency practitioners will be seeking their pound of flesh before all creditors, and if they do not see substantial assets or liquid funds, they may well decline to act for a company and guide it through a CVL, therefore its liquidation will be undertaken by necessity through the Official Receiver.

Whichever type of 'funeral' your debtor is involved with, the order for priority when it comes to the payment of creditors is the same.

First come the **secured creditors**, probably a bank with a debenture (mortgage) being a fixed and floating charge. If the fixed charge has been exceeded and therefore the 'floating charge' invoked, then the balance covered by the floating charge is dropped in priority to behind the next group of creditors, the **preferential creditors**. These include the Inland Revenue, Customs and Excise, and arrears of wages and holiday pay. There are also a few rather more obscure bodies from the EEC covered by this heading. The **floating charge** holder now takes centre stage, likely to be a financial institution of one type or another.

Unfortunately, last but one on the list and often the most severely affected by company insolvency – and so often forced to follow suit themselves – are the **unsecured creditors**.

The **shareholders** come in last of all – maybe it's seen as a punishment for what is considered as gambling on a company's prospects, or as par for the course for the risk-takers!

Other terms you might come across when dealing with insolvency are:

- **Shadow director** This is someone who is not a company director, but on occasion advises, instructs or directs the directors of a company and whose advice is generally accepted. Many of the obligations and responsibilities associated with directorship also apply to shadow directors. A major shareholder or perhaps even a banker could be a shadow director.
- **Wrongful trading** This occurs when a company director knows or should have known that insolvency was inevitable and yet continued trading to the detriment of the creditors. The directors can be found liable personally for any losses incurred by creditors unless they can show that they took 'every step' to minimise the losses.

● **Fraudulent trading** Until the introduction of the term 'wrongful trading' by the 1986 Insolvency Act, this was virtually the only course of action that could be taken against a director and required stringent levels of evidence to prove intent to cause losses to creditors. It leans heavily towards criminal rather than civil law and can result in imprisonment.

USEFUL ADDRESSES AND CONTACTS

I have noted below some of the many organisations, firms and individuals who have provided me with assistance and information concerning insolvency. Although I have tried to restrict it to those with information relevant to a frustrated creditor rather than to an aspiring author, inevitably these overlap at times. However, it is worth browsing through if your interest in insolvency has not diminished!

Association of British Factors and Discounters
1 Northumberland Avenue
London WC2N 5BW
(071)-930-9112

A trade association with most of the biggest and best known companies in the field counted as their members. Advice and information on factoring in general and lists of members available.

Association of British Insurers
51 Gresham Street
London EC2V 7HQ
(071)-600-3333

Worth contacting if you are considering credit insurance or perhaps insuring yourself as a director against an action brought under the Insolvency Act

Citizens Advice Bureaux
You will often find your local CAB situated close to the library and it will be listed in the phone book. My local branch assured me that they would all have access to expert advice from someone within the field of insolvency and are always willing to help. Remember they are often busy and phone lines are frequently engaged. I dropped a letter in personally and waited until they rang me in the end!

Companies House
Postal Search Section
Crown Way
Cardiff CF4 BUZ
(0222)-380801

Invaluable source of information on past debtors or future customers. Either contact them direct or via one of the many agents.

Cork Gully
Shelley House
3 Noble Street
London EC2V 7DQ
(071)-606-7700

Insolvency Practitioners

Forum of Private Business
Ruskin Chambers
Drury Lane
Knutsford
Cheshire WA16 5HA
(0565)-634467

Insolvency Service
Bridge Place
88/89 Eccleston Square
London SW1V 1PT

The Insolvency Service is 'an Executive Agency within the Department of Trade and Industry'. It is a useful source of information for general queries or for specific aspects of your insolvent debtor. Don't expect to get the same person twice, though, and don't expect a swift answer. I have found that they tend to reply to me in 'politician's lingo' — a lot of words that seem to be less than specific as a rule!

The Insolvency Service Disqualification Unit
Room 513
address as above

This is where you should address any information or details you may have concerning your insolvent debtor if you believe that there is cause for investigation. Until you can establish the name of the examiner handling the case, simply address it to 'Senior Examiner'.

Institute of Credit Management
The Watermill
South Lussenham
Oakham
Leics. LE15 8NB
(0780)-721888

Useful trade association, who can provide you with advice and information. They run training seminars to promote the effectiveness of their industry.

International Factors Limited
Joan Rafferty
Marketing Dept.
International Factors Limited
Sovereign House
Church Street
Brighton BN1 3WX

International Factors Limited has produced a 20 minute video on factoring, which is available free of charge from Joan Rafferty at the address above. Please state whether you require VHS or BETA.

KPMG Peat Marwick
Corporate Recovery
P.O. Box 730
20 Farringdon Street
London EC4A 4PP
(071)-236-8000

They provide a useful guide to the new insolvency laws, although it seems to be aimed more at the specialist rather than the man in the street. One of the senior partners, John Alexander, was extremely helpful in the preparation of this book.

Library

Your local library may well have some useful text, and will certainly have the actual relevant Acts of Parliament we have looked at in this book. The librarians are usually only too pleased to be given a challenge and all my local ones have spent many happy hours searching for anything concerning insolvency — usually to no avail. There are various books, though, that can be obtained through the central library service at your local library if you are interested in the finer details of insolvency law, one of which is *Insolvency* by Harry Rajak, who is probably one of the most knowledgeable people in the field and a source of great support to me during the writing of this book!

Occupational Pensions Advisory Service (OPAS)

11 Belgrave Road
London SW1V 1RB
(071)-233-8080

Very helpful service for anyone with pension problems, including those who have pensions with insolvent companies. They have a drastically increased workload due to changes in government legislation concerning the Social Security Act and the Pensions Ombudsman.

Office of the Banking Ombudsman

Citadel House
5—11 New Fetter Lane
London EC4A 1BR

Worth contacting if you have problems concerning your own bank; however, they will not be interested if you have a complaint about the behaviour of your debtor's bankers, because they will only consider complaints between customers and their own bankers. The Chartered Institute of Bankers are also worth a quick call if only to try and point you in another direction.

Political parties

Apart from contacting your own local MP, it is probably worthwhile writing to the Minister for Corporate Affairs at the Department of Trade and Industry, Ashdown House, 123 Victoria Street,

SW1E 6RB. If your own MP is worth his salt and particularly if he happens to belong to the party in power, he will very likely write to him on your behalf anyway.

For the purposes of this book, I contacted just about every relevant Tory from the Prime Minister downwards — who incidentally wrote back to me virtually by return of post. I also corresponded with a helpful Liberal MP whose particular field of interest is the law. However, despite three letters, I never actually managed to stir the Labour party into action.

Society of Practitioners of Insolvency (SPI)
18–19 Long Lane
London, EC1
(071)-600-3375

A useful source of general information particularly for selecting a practitioner. They also publish a glossary of insolvency expressions.

Turpin Barker & Armstrong
Brittingham House
Orchart Street
Crawley
Sussex RH11 7AE
(0293)-549866

Certainly not one of the larger firms, but one that I found to be particularly helpful. Mr Mundy was probably the first insolvency professional to take the time to sit down with me and answer all my questions with patience.

The following organisations might be worth contacting depending on your particular needs and interests. I made contact with all of them during the course of writing this book, but would not necessarily have found them particularly helpful if I was only concerned with our particular debtor.

Institute of Directors — (071)-839-1233 — They have a small team of consultants specialising in various subjects including insolvency, who are available for consultation by members by appointment.

The Law Society — (071)-242-1222 — Useful starting point for advice or in your search for a legal viewpoint.

CBI — (071)-379-7400

Association of British Chambers of Commerce — (071)-240-5831 — useful for statistics, trends and analysis as they publish some of the DTI figures amongst others.

Registry Trust Ltd
173 Cleveland St
London W1P 5PE
(071)-380-0133

If you are a member of a trade organisation or association, union or federation, then most certainly contact the information department. Some can be more helpful than others depending on the requirements of their members and funds available.

I made contact with all the major High Street Banks concerning this book and found them all offering similar advice — and mostly promoting their own allied services. But you would probably be very wise to discuss matters in detail with your bank manager. At the end of the day, much will depend on the individual manager and the sort of relationship you have with him. Never be taken by surprise lest they leave you up the proverbial creek — paddleless!

Footnote: I did contact the Office of Fair Trading concerning in particular the directors of the insolvent company I was dealing with and also their bankers. I was told — and I quote — that '*The Office of Fair Trading is actually nothing to do with fair trading*'. They felt they were unable to help me; I *knew* they were!

INDEX

Administration Orders 40, 81, 130
Administrative Receivership 45, 81, 84, 114, 129
Administrator 42, 84, 131
Association of British Factors and Discounters 98, 135

bankruptcy
  personal 16, 25, 72, 74
  petition 10
  trustee 74
bailiffs 10

Charging Order 11, 15, 21
Citizens Advice Bureau 35, 54
Companies House 18, 42, 50, 65, 86, 117
Company Voluntary Arrangements (CVAs) 20, 51, 81, 131
contingency fees 122
County Court 10, 72
Cork Committee 33, 59
credit
  checking agencies 3, 96
  control 2, 92, 100
  controllers 2, 3, 12, 95
  insurance 96, 99
  references 93
creditors
  committee 44, 48
  meeting 18, 48, 51, 55
  power 15
  preferential 130, 133
  report to 50, 84
  secured 12, 130, 133
  unsecured 20, 38, 42, 46, 50, 70, 130, 133

debt
  debtors lists 2
  collection agencies 5, 7, 8, 12

Department of Trade and Industry (DTI) 20, 25, 61, 64, 73
directors
  disqualification of 33, 59, 81, 91
  Institute of 35
  shadow 33, 65, 127, 133

factoring 27, 97
Federation of Small Businesses 35
Forum of Private Business 125
fraudulent trading 24, 33, 59, 69, 134

Garnishee 11, 15, 21

High Court 10

insolvency
  Act 10, 13, 16, 17, 33, 60, 65
  Practitioner 13, 24, 32, 34, 56, 66, 73, 131
  Service 61, 81, 89, 129
Institute of Chartered Accountants 14
Institute of Credit Management 96

judgement 9, 12, 21

Law Society 14, 33
liquidation
  Compulsory 53, 129
  Creditors Voluntary 17, 19, 54, 70, 72, 132
  Members Voluntary 53, 132
lien 15, 22

Official Receiver 64, 68, 74, 81, 121, 129, 133
Ombudsman
  banking 113

partnerships 26, 76, 99, 123
pensions 39, 138
preference 16

Retention of Title 15, 22

Society of Practitioners in Insolvency 14, 61
Statutory Demands 10, 11, 31
Summary Judgements 11

winding up 10, 13, 41, 56, 66, 132
Wrongful Trading 24, 32, 34, 60, 67, 71, 82, 133